THE WONDER
OF PRAYER

THE
WONDER
OF
PRAYER

—

by Shelton Hale Bishop

Foreword by Austin Pardue

GREENWICH · CONNECTICUT

1959

TO my Mother, deepest inspiration of my life, in Paradise more than 60 years now, drawing me always closer to Him; and to my daughters, Beth and Eloise, whose love and faith in their difficult father have always helped to bind me to my Lord.

FOREWORD

I can visualize *The Wonder of Prayer* resting on the night table next to many a bed. But it will do more than rest, for it will be read. Perhaps only a few minutes at a time and probably not every night; but it will be a companion to many at moments when they need more than a few routine bedtime prayers.

Books of meditation and devotion can only be written out of long personal search for the Peace of God. Only such searching can give validity to these books.

The Wonder of Prayer comes from the heart of a man who has acquired knowledge of his subject through the discipline and practice of the art of prayer. As you read it you will grow in a sense of awareness, not only of the Presence of God, but in the reality of the experience of the writer. He has undoubtedly searched the classical literature in the field of mystical theology, but you may be sure that he has inwardly digested it.

Shelton Hale Bishop is qualified to write this book because he has long been one of America's outstanding parish priests. As rector of the largest Episcopal Church in New York City, he has had a vast experience in the cure of souls. Few men in the

United States have seen as much in the way of spiritual counseling as has Shelton Bishop during his incumbency at St. Philip's. He has ministered to intellectual leaders in medicine, law, commerce, and the arts as well as to juvenile delinquents, alcoholics, prostitutes, and the destitute.

Shelton Bishop has technically retired although he is as active today as he was in the parish harness. He just does different things. Furthermore, he is still a young man in body and spirit. He is vital, alive, and strong. He communicates in depth and simplicity. His book will help you to grow in grace, wisdom, and the understanding of God and man.

AUSTIN PARDUE

PREFACE

ARE there many things in life
more wonderful than a truly intimate talk with someone whom
we have long loved or whom we came to love through Christ
in a moment? I have had many such experiences of communion
—at one time with a cherished friend, at another with someone
whom I had never seen or known previously. In both cases power,
understanding, and a strange spiritual flame lit the interior way;
truth and meaning came "out of the clear"; and life took a new
stance and prospect. So it can be with prayer, too.

Any valuable book about prayer is a revealing story of spiritual
experience. It tells what the writer knows about that communication which goes on between God and human beings. It has to be
a revelation of the personal experience that the Holy Spirit has
given the writer directly, as well as the record of what he has
humbly learned from others. One can offer such a book to others
only with humility and the hope that it will help renew the
reader's desire for a life with God in Christ through prayer.

My grateful appreciation goes to the Reverend Dr. M. Moran
Weston, my friend and successor at St. Philip's Church, New
York City, for his encouragement to write and for his care and

9

patience in reading and helping edit the final draft of the manuscript. And also to Mrs. Beatrice Goris, who graciously typed the original manuscript. And finally, to the hundreds of young girls who, through thirteen years of the Northfield Conferences, allowed me to reveal to them "the wonder of prayer." Scripture quotations are from the Revised Standard Version of the Bible (copyright 1946 and 1952).

S. H. B.

CONTENTS

Foreword 7

Preface 9

1 Basis 15

2 Practice 28

3 Struggle 41

4 Failure 55

5 Power 68

6 Peace 82

THE WONDER
OF PRAYER

1 · BASIS

How it was we first began to pray is always interesting to recall. In my own case, there are not many things that I remember about my early years, but, strangely enough, about my first prayers I have a vivid remembrance. It was my mother who taught me to pray. There were six of us children, and my brother and I shared a bedroom together. Every night, and I mean *every* night, when we were ready "to jump in," Mother came to our room, knelt down between us—always between us—and we quietly and reverently talked with God. She always ended our prayer by singing the hymn,

> Jesus, tender Shepherd, hear me;
> Bless thy little lamb tonight . . .

in which we joined. Then she kissed both of us before we got off our knees, and that was "Good Night."

This recollection is one of those precious things in life that never leaves one: the special time every day when the one we loved best helped us to speak with, and learn to know better, Him who loves us best.

God is our Father! How many times have we heard that said, and said it ourselves. But never let that thought become a commonplace, for Jesus has made it the key to all our praying. "Our Father." This is the blessed Name with which to begin praying. Its invocation is most natural, for the man who does not know his father is rudderless. Too many children today suffer that misery. But almost in worse plight is the lad who knows his father only to apologize for him or to despise him or, most regretfully, to hate him. A life that has known this kind of deprivation poses inner problems that can probably never be altogether mastered. Father-love is, indeed, the other side of mother-love, and poor is the person who has not known both in happy concord. It is normal, then, that we should be directed first to Him who is "God and Father of us all" (*Ephesians* 4:6) when we need help from beyond. "When you pray, say 'Our Father.'" (*Luke* 11:2)

When we reach out for something we do not have, for some real help, we need to reach out to someone who stands in a special relation to us. When we need care, counsel, food, medicine or money, we usually turn to someone whose attitude is cordial and whose favorable response we can count on. God has a very special relation to us. And that assurance is a necessary one for us to start with. It is impossible for us to think of God, as Christ has revealed Him to us, without recognizing that He loves us. So many people are accustomed to say this with their lips and to hear it with their ears, but at the same time never to let its full meaning sink into their hearts.

That God loves us is the true basis of all that life means. Not to know love, not to know that someone, somewhere, loves us, is to have an emptiness at the core of our very being for which nothing compensates. The misery of people who have no one to love them, who cannot turn to one person who has for them a continuing regard, steadfast trust, affectionate good will, and wholesome respect, is real torture. On the other hand, to know that parent or child, mate or friend, is always there when one needs him— this assurance provides life with a solid and substantial base.

OUR FATHER

This depth of meaning, I believe, is to be found in the words "Our Father." We are made of divine stuff, "in His image." It is only the perverted father, or the utterly irresponsible one, who is without love for the offspring of his loins. But there are many gradations of love, and the most faithful father is one that loves most faithfully. Jesus drew a picture of this for us. "Bring quickly the best robe, and put it on him; and put a ring on his hand, and shoes on his feet"—that son of his must have been a pitiful sight —"and bring the fatted calf and kill it, and let us eat and make merry; for this my son was dead and is alive again; he was lost and is found." (*Luke* 15:22-24)

Certainly this is an extreme example, as anyone knows who has faced a similar situation either on a natural level without the benefit of religious conviction, or on a spiritual level when, for example, despite his prayer, he is summoned to court because of charges against his son, or when he has had his fifteen- or sixteen-year-old daughter stand before him "in trouble." Yet this extreme example is the one our Lord uses to show us our Father's love. *God loves absolutely, no matter what.* No human loves absolutely. We seem to do so only provided the depths of our being and our love are not tried too sorely. God's love has no breaking point. If we turn to Him in disgust and revolt at the mire into which we have sunk—the mire of pride and distaste for life until nothing matters, or of passion, greed, and cruelty that kill while they are fed—His love seems even greater because of the very grievousness of our sin and wickedness. The Cross of Christ makes this fact undeniable, and St. Paul spells it out for us: "God shows his love for us in that while we were yet sinners Christ died for us." (*Romans* 5:8)

There is no such love as this, save in God. And this is the kind of love that draws us to Him. Love always draws; this is its power. In Ripley's *Believe It or Not* awhile back, there was a pen sketch of an enormous vacuum cleaner mounted on a 25-ton truck to suck up everything "from pebbles to lost wrenches" along the runway so that the jet engines would not pick them up. How shall we ever understand that such is the love of God, in our Lord Jesus, that draws all evil out of us into Himself and thereby makes us feel the glorious pull of our hearts into His? This is a wondrous power, one finally well-nigh irresistible.

Love draws and pursues. The true father will not hesitate, if it seems wise strategy, to go after his son in the most delicate, persuasive, or determined way. This is to him an inseparable part of steadfast love. He cannot wait for one of his children to return: he goes "to seek and to save." (*Luke* 19:10) It is even possible to think of him snatching and rescuing.

Only the other day a man was driving his car slowly down hill on a dead-end street. Two women were standing at the foot talking, as housewives will in the morning. Quite suddenly one of them broke away and ran ahead of the car into the driveway where the car would turn. When it reached the turn, there was the mother, her two-year-old snatched up into her arms, coming back out into the narrow street.

Think of the elements of communication in this seemingly simple human situation! An oncoming car, a two-year-old un- aware, a mother's haste to gather her child out of danger, the threat to the child's life on one level and hers on another, and her rapture when she faces the driver, her child saved. A simple, any-day, human situation, yet filled with the elements of life any of us could, if we would, find in our extraordinary life with God. *The wonder of it!*

What keeps a good many people away from real prayer is the fact that they do not *know* God. Prayer, however, requires that we understand where we are going and to whom. When Jesus calls God "Father," and bids us approach Him as "our Father," He puts His finger on our hearts in a telling way. He interprets for us God's love. For the very name "father" presents an image that every language, every culture, every condition can comprehend. Anyone with a normal family experience can appreciate and, at least partly, understand this robust, strong, persuasive image.

God, then, is our Father—Father in a sense we never fully understand. The only way we can catch even a glimpse of what God is, is to look at His Son and what His Son has told us about Him. "I and the Father are one"; "The Father is in me and I in the Father"; "He who has seen me has seen the Father." (*John* 10:30; *ibid.* 10:38; *ibid.* 14:8)

When we pray, we need this compelling assurance that God is our Father. It was to His heavenly Father Jesus directed His prayers and He bids us to do the same. There is something totally encompassing about the Father's relationship to us and ours to Him. For the Father has a total concern for everything in the universe, and for every moment of the life of everything that exists—and that includes the total life of every human being, with respect to both sin and the beat of his heart, to both his attempts at space travel and his finding an adequate place to park. Our Father's caring cannot be ignored; it demands response. But it also makes response difficult; for, implicit in His care and love, is His judgment, under which we stand.

OUR JUDGE

Love inspires the loved one to measure up to its demands. We need only to think of human love. An integral part of the response of anyone to simple kindness is, "How do I deserve this? I am not worthy." We want to lift ourselves to a new level where at least we can return in some way the spirit of the kindness bestowed. We judge ourselves unworthy even to receive the tray of nourishment that a friend unexpectedly brings to our sick-bed, one such as only prayerful consideration could have prepared. "Oh! you are so wonderful; but you should not have done that!" Sincere this is, and out of a heart that knows how frequently it has failed in any similar gesture.

This is real communication—communion, if you will. Two people reacting toward each other from different vantage points: one showing love, pure and simple; the other accepting graciously that token of love and, in the light of it, experiencing a sense of unworthiness. This is what it means to be under the judgment of love.

This, then, makes the Father a different kind of judge. God *is* our Judge, and not one of us can escape His judgment. Yet, Christ has made it eminently clear that our first approach to God is in response to His love and trust. This is our primary, pure response to anybody who does not set up in us a feeling of fear. If we do not know the love of God, either superficially or deeply, we shall never really pray. Prayer grows feeble when love for Him fades. Real communion rests ultimately on love. This is its primary basis.

But this very fact also sets up a reaction that seems to contradict the first. The perfect love of God makes us conscious of all our imperfection. At the same time, however, it suggests that we could be perfected if God were given a free hand in us through Christ—His power and His grace. This is the judgment of God upon us.

This, then, is the second basis upon which true prayer life is built: the judgment of God within us. It is with us almost every moment, but not always, thank God, consciously. Our conscience presents it to us at moments of choice, decision, and temptation; at times of moral and spiritual failure, as well as of guilt, pain, suffering, and death. In their struggle with the temptations and the moral choices they have to make, men turn somewhere for guidance and help. They may draw on the resources of their own characters, or on the love and loyalty of family, or on their position in society. But wherever they turn, the point is that they inevitably measure their decision against how it will affect others, how they will be judged. At such moments of decision the believing and worshipping person actually stands before God, before the One who has cared for him and defended him; and after he stacks up all that God is, all that He has been able to reveal in the redeeming love of Jesus, he lays this beside all that tempts him away from his Father. This is the great area of prayer. This is that fateful transaction between God Almighty and the human soul in crisis.

Pity the man or nation that does not know in such instances of life that God is the Judge.

> Once to every man and nation
> Comes the moment to decide . . .
> Then it is the brave man chooses
> While the coward stands aside.

This is the marvelous miracle of life when we are conscious—one would almost dare to say, spiritually conscious—that it is God in Christ who is judging us. Do you shy away from believing this? Think for a moment: Do not fathers, mothers, friends, *out of deepest, purest love,* stand to judge those committed to them for their good? Does not a doctor or a captain of a ship have to assume the role of judge? What we should hope for is that their judgments be faultless. But that is what always, at all times, under all circumstances, characterizes the judgment of our Father's love, and of Christ's love, and of the Spirit's guidance. With God always, "mercy triumphs over judgment," "for his judgments are true and just." (*James* 2:13; *Rev.* 19:2)

In prayer God's law—His will and purpose—is brought ever more vividly before us. What we need to be sure of, in order to rely completely on Him and follow Him obediently, is that *His Father-love and His just judgment are not only inseparably woven together but are revealed to us in every particular situation that arises.* This is true whether we turn to Him for strength to accept or to resist, whether we choose to go it alone or to company with Him. Yet, experience teaches us that when we take Him into our confidence and admit Him into the arena of our moral strivings, He confronts us with His values, His love, His justice, His purity, His faithfulness, and His promises. He gives us the wonderful vision of how it will be if we give Him consent and, at the same time, a clear, though by no means complete, picture of our confusion and defeat if we deny Him.

Nobody can truly understand the basis of prayer until he has plumbed the depths of this kind of relationship with God. While few of us address ourselves to God as Judge, none escapes judgment in any phase of life. Men are always judging—distance, strength, weight, reaction, and quality. We may be forbidden to judge our neighbor, but mostly to our sorrow—and often to our regret—we can't help ourselves. That is how deep judging goes in all of us, and also, by instinct, in every one of God's creatures. While the horse is being judged for merit, he is judging the distance to the bar he must clear to bring his master the blue ribbon. Shall we believe that man, in the moral and spiritual sphere of human activity, can possibly avoid the judgment of God in all his relationships?

But there is a constructive side to this: The judgment of God is woven into the texture of our very being so that God Himself can bring His love into our failure and turn it to our well-being. Anyone of experience can testify how wonderful it is that, in the long run, faithful, painstaking prayer gives us clear access to the knowledge of God's will for us, the strength and desire to do what He wants us to do, and the increased capacity—which we call blessing—to persist in well-doing, to find great satisfaction in it, and finally to love it because it is God's will, not ours alone.

JESUS—THE MAN OF PRAYER

It is in Christ Jesus that we find the best example of how we are to pray. Jesus prayed; He prayed constantly; He was continuously in touch with His Father. And if we are to understand prayer at all, we must understand what "in touch with" means. Jesus was always conscious of God's presence and, at the same time, immediately conscious of the life and need of every man. How quickly He could relate Himself to everyone, and everyone to Himself and to His Father. It might be the woman at the well, or the rich young ruler, or the centurion; or it might be the widow whose son was being borne to his burial, a group of children, demoniacs, or a cripple. Their cry of need excited His full compassion, and in a moment He was so closely in touch with them that His power met their need in ways beyond their knowing. And whatever the spiritual encounter, one feels it was His touch with God that directed it.

At every moment He was Lord and Saviour. He had the Father's love, and the mercy of His judgment, always in His heart and at His finger tips. *The source of all His concern for man, and His power to bring God straight into men's lives, lay in His assurance that God was in Him.* This was the secret of His power. The fact that He drew on it, that He was continuously in touch with Power and Love that gave Him power and love, brought all those who were in touch with Him into contact with God. Those who received Him felt another presence. Those who became hostile were brought under judgment, and one such "went and hanged himself." (*Matthew* 27:05; *ibid.* 26:25)

Men did not understand this nearness of God in their lives until Jesus revealed it. Not that men had not previously prayed—all men pray after one fashion or another. But the assurance that God is everywhere immediately present, that God is the source of every one of life's secrets, and ready to help and to rule in every situation—it was Jesus alone who conveyed this actuality in His very life. He had to face treachery, denunciation, insult, accusation, and death at the hands of men. And yet, in all these situations, He fulfilled the purpose for which God gave Him life: "God . . . gave his only Son that whoever believes in him should not perish." (*John* 3:16) At every moment Jesus *is* Lord and Saviour.

To know that there is One who saves, and saves completely, sends men flying to Him. Generations upon generations of people have believed and have been saved from all manner of failure and sin because Jesus' promise of unfailing salvation has been the basis of their trust in Him. They have poured out to Him and to the Father, in His Name, their pleas for mercy and support, for forgiveness and healing, and for the renewal of their lives.

Christians pray *because* of Christ Jesus. He is their example; but, most of all, He is their hope and their salvation. It is so necessary to see that *He* prayed. The New Testament story is full of references to His prayer-life. The impact of that life on His disciples is suggested by their request for instruction in prayer: "He was praying in a certain place and when he ceased, one of his disciples said to him, 'Lord, teach us to pray.'" (*Luke* 11:1) Here was the example. It could not have been just the form, the posture of His praying. It was certainly that—for they would not have noticed any prayer that did not have some outward expression—a bowed head and bended knees in a place apart, studied silence, and a reverent attitude. But it was a great deal more; it was a relationship with God which He revealed. "When you pray, go into your room and shut the door and pray to your Father who is in secret." "And when he had dismissed the crowds, he went up into the hills by himself to pray." (*Matthew* 6:6; 14:23)

There can be no doubt that Jesus is "the Man of Prayer" for all ages. But the real reason Christians pray is not that Jesus is our example in prayer, but that He is the Saviour of the world, of everyone in the world who turns to Him.

SOMEONE WHO CAN SAVE

This is the picture that men have of God: Someone who can save—from desolation, from destruction, from death. Prayer is not always a cry issuing from helplessness or aimlessness, from doubt or desperation. It may be the humble acknowledgment of a Being who is *other* than they, upon whom they can depend, to whom they can lift up their hearts and their voices in praise and adoration. Prayer can be like the appreciative messages men send to other men who have achieved distinction, exhibited great prowess, performed some feat or humane service. This kind of acknowledgment is universal. We see it follow upon achievement at a circus, or in the field of science, art or literature, or in some great adventure or deed of bravery and sacrifice. Why should men not do the same in response to the Supreme Hero, the Performer without human equal, the Spirit that transcends every human arrangement and relationship?

This is what, I believe, people mean when they say that every man prays. I know an avowed agnostic, a commercial pilot, a wonderful husband, and father of handsome children. He is also a conscientious and devoted leader of a Cub Pack and Boy Scout Troop, exerting wholesome character-building influence on the boys. He is quiet, persuasive, and commanding. The authority he wields is something wonderful to watch. He would say he does not pray. But what else is this loving concern for the development of each individual boy as though he were his own flesh and blood? He does not pretend to have the formula for the over-all growth of these boys into fine manhood. But he cares supremely; his whole bearing is that of one who believes that there is a standard, a caring, a power that is beyond us and toward which we reach. Of course this is presumption, but it is the kind of presumption scientists lay such store by, and explorers, and all serious adventurers in life. Their presumption may be vain, but how else does one find a new land, or the cure for disease, or hidden gold? Men always seek that which is beyond themselves and believe it is there to be found. Often they believe that even the effort is sufficient reward. The experience itself excites joy and gratitude. It is a form of salvation.

No matter what our development may be, or what the character of our lives, the essence of salvation appears to be woven into prayer. If I adore another human being, my spirit says with rapture that the person I adore has been saved from being less than he might have been. If I praise, I see something that might have been much more, but escapes being less. If I give thanks, it is because someone did not fail. This is our experience.

25

Salvation, too, is part of the very structure of the relationship man has with his God. That is why Jesus is the perfect revelation of God. God saves. With all the destruction and death that there is in nature, God *conserves* enough for the maintenance of human life—enough of light and energy, of food and water, of beauty and variety. Say what you will, He continues to save in abundance that which He has made. It is wrought into His very being. And, much of the time, man is somehow reaching out in great ignorance and wilfulness toward this "divine strain," trusting to it, depending upon it, consciously and unconsciously drawing upon the certainty of it to balance his innate insecurity and lack.

When Jesus says, "God sent the Son into the world, not to condemn the world, but that the world might be saved through him (*John* 3:17)," He is speaking primarily of that inner world of which the Collect says "we have no power of *ourselves* to help ourselves." "I can will what is right," says St. Paul, "but I cannot do it. For I do not do the good I want, but the evil I do not want is what I do." (*Romans* 7:18-19)

We shall have to face this basic conflict in man's life later on, but now we need only to say that the hope we have of being saved in this situation—and every man is in exactly the same predicament as St. Paul—is that Jesus saves. Automatically? As by magic, as soon as we become helpless? Hardly. The admission of our plight, the recourse we know we have to One who saves, this is the encounter of man with God. God is in Christ—is seen, and known, to be in Him. And the soul turns in its need and pleads gently or desperately for the saving power it does not have "of itself" but seeks "in Jesus." This is the reason we "bow our knees before the Father" in and "through Jesus Christ our Lord." (*Ephesians* 3:14)

Not that all turn to Jesus. But there is the same need of salvation for all, no matter where they turn. Ignorance, failure, obstruction, sickness, separation, and sin stalk each one of us. We reach out for relief, for release, for renewal, and we cannot find it in ourselves, nor adequately in any of the race of men, all

26

similarly afflicted as we are. It is to our Elder Brother, One like ourselves, but with none of our limitations, to whom we turn, One who is beyond and above us, but has suffered and died "for us men and for our salvation." (Nicene Creed)

THE TRUE BASIS OF PRAYER

This, then, is where we must start if we would pray. Behind every activity of man, there is a basis of operation. This basis as presented here is theological, some will say. Without doubt! All life stems from God. That makes it theological. We do not usually describe it that way. We prefer to call it natural. But nature is of God and of God alone. He has made all things. It happens that "the Maker of all things" is also "the Father Almighty" and "the Judge of all men" and has made Himself known to us perfectly in His Son, Jesus Christ, the Saviour of the world.

In this faith prayer is born. It may be only a whisper, a lifting of the eyes, a sense of beauty, of goodness, of truth, for which there is a slight, indefinable yearning. Why? on what basis? for what reason? to what purpose? We don't know; only something stirs within us and we "feel after" that which seems to be outside of us. With "which"—no, it must be with *whom* we can make contact. That there will be a response, an answering "feel," a touch, is our scarcely recognizable hope. But it is there; and we have made a beginning, the beginning of a conscious, sure approach to God—and some dim recognition of the approach that God is trying to make to us. Then we have found the true basis for prayer—it has been made known to us. There is a call in it, and we are moved to respond.

2 · PRACTICE

W<small>E ARE</small> all children of God, children of the one Father. But children have a great deal to learn, and learning often is not easy. Ignorance, resistance, ingrained curiosity, the lure of the new, yet fear of the unknown and the untried—all make for the problems and conflicts that accompany this process.

Communication is one area of life in which these problems and conflicts are especially manifest. It is not always easy to convey to another all that one desires to convey, or to receive clearly, in turn, what others are communicating. This is a problem of prayer, too, and it is one, if not the chief, reason why we require symbols —movements, posture, words, pictures, objects, tokens—to achieve in our worship vivid, living communication with God. To call God "Father," to envision the Cross, to kneel, to use water, and bread and wine as we do—all are human efforts to reach out toward the Divine, and to make vivid and living to ourselves the invisible One and His attributes.

All this is part of "the practice of religion." For religion, too, has to have its methods of learning and nurture. Now prayer is an essential method of learning and nurture in that total relationship to God we call "religion." We could well argue that since every relationship requires some kind of communication, prayer must be looked upon as fundamental to our communication with God.

As everybody knows, there are levels of communication and varying degrees of proficiency at each level. We ought especially to remember this when we think about prayer. Duke Ellington, Leonard Bernstein, Handel, and Mozart communicate to us on different levels; only a few question the ability of any one of them to communicate. But no one would deny that their proficiency in communicating came to them only after long, arduous application to, and practice in, their art.

Prayer can be no different. The prayers of the saints mark the highest reaches of the soul in its striving toward perfection in the art of Christian living. We know something of the discipline and the time, the separation on the one hand, and the identification with people in their struggles on the other, that went into the saints' practice of prayer. The lives of the saints, recorded in such detail, testify to that.

It is not likely that this writer, or most of his readers, will ever reach the devotional level of the saints in prayer. Many, to be sure, will desire to improve and bring to greater perfection "the gifts of the Spirit" they already have received. But to do that requires practice. It demands separation, and it requires "assembling of ourselves together"—contradictory as this may seem. Jesus withdrew time and time again from the multitude and from His companions to go apart "into the hills" to pray. (*Matthew* 14:23; see also *Mark* 6:46 and *Luke* 6:12.) The Gospels all record this. But it is recorded that He frequently prayed in the company of large numbers of people, under widely varying circumstances and, importantly, that He joined in the worship of the people who gathered together in the local synagogues. Here is the twofold practice which should characterize prayer life—a life that is lived apart *from* involvement, yet derives its meaning from the experience *of* involvement with the lives of others.

APART FOR GOD

God has to be seen apart from everything in the world. He is in the world, but not of the world. He is holy. Nothing in the world is holy except as God gives it its separate and distinctive relationship to Himself. The holy of holies, whether it be the sanctuary of a church or the sanctuary of one's heart, is something separate and set apart for God.

Prayer has to be an activity carried on apart with God—an activity, directed toward God, of the heart, mind, soul, and, I think, of the body, too. This is very difficult to achieve. We are easily distracted. We are all prone to become so entangled in our own affairs that we cannot tear ourselves away from them. Therefore, everyone has to learn to practice concentration.

So, for prayer, we shut ourselves off. We seek a quiet place where sight, sound, and movement are at a minimum. Life today has become such that we have to will this experience, to struggle for this minimal condition. At first, our span of continuity will probably be short, just as it is with the beginner at the piano, for example. Interest, caring, love as well as skill, however, develop only through continued practice. If we have any real love for the thing at which we work, wonderfully rewarding attitudes, as well as performance, will be achieved. One of the secrets of success is the discipline we impose in separating ourselves from all distracting pressures. There is power in being alone to work at one's task. It is important "to shut the door," as Jesus said, "and pray to your Father who is in secret." (*Matthew* 6:6)

The intimacies of life play a large and important part in prayer. There are two intimacies in prayer that we must note: the intimacy of one's own knowledge of God in Christ Jesus, one's faith and trust and love, none of which can ever be revealed completely to anyone else; and the intimacy of one's own secret self, distinctive, unique, and very personal. This is our secret with God and God's secret knowledge and love for us. Lovers need always to be apart with their love, whether it be in the family relationship or in courtship. Even the child acknowledges this need for intimacy—when he begins to pray, he wants to say his prayers alone his own way.

This, then, is the beginning of our practice in prayer. The more we love to pray, the more real our communication with God becomes, the more we shall need time and space to be "alone with God." Physical separation needs to be emphasized, for without it, separation of other kinds is made more difficult.

Hectic absorption is the bane of our complex society and complicated lives. Few of us escape it. Yet it is one of the great enemies of the soul, for we shall never have time for God unless we *make* that time. How many of us make it a part of the cultivation of the best in life to heed God's call, to give Him a part of every day, in order to absorb the wonders of His glory, to spell out to Him our spiritual needs and failures? It is not merely a matter of schedule, though that is a consideration. *It is chiefly a matter of practice.* Prayer is something we have to stay at, for prayer is an art. Those of us who really cherish our religion are bound to acknowledge this. We cannot give ourselves to every demand of the moment, no matter how innocent or innocuous it may appear, and at the same time experience the growing power of prayer and the wonders it can work in the whole of life.

Set apart a space in each day for God. Do not be anxious about what will happen. If you want to learn to drive a car, you set apart a period of time each day or each week, and the person who is going to teach you will take care of the details. You have to have the desire, the separation from everything else, and the commitment of yourself to the person who knows how to handle the machine expertly.

Anyone experienced in prayer knows that you can learn to pray, and learn to love it and to revel in the wonders it opens and the relationship that comes to be established through it with God and His world, with people and things. A time, a place, separated for Him and toward Him! Regularly? Continuously? Consistently?

For the rest of your life? Yes—and nothing short of that! In this demand prayer does not differ from love. Do you put love off and on? If so, it is no more love—any more than is character when put off. Indeed, anyone who does not think it necessary to practice all the niceties, all the delicate fringe things of love to keep it the most vital and vibrantly joyous experience of life does not understand the simple spiritual mechanics of living.

It is this way with prayer, too. Prayer has to occupy a continuous part in our life. It has to be practiced constantly. And the tools of prayer are *love, quiet, separateness to God*—even though sometimes only for a moment—*faithfulness, earnestness, mostly kneeling, a special intention, and words.*

WORDS

This last we have to consider seriously. It is not possible to think without words. The words may never be uttered, but they have to be there. It is a difficult thing to propose, but you may not be conscious of the words as words. Nevertheless they are there, and they are there in a more or less orderly construction. We have to think in sentences, complete sentences, broken sentences, phrase after phrase evolving, intruding itself, flooding in.

Words are our chief means of communication. Very few Christians have yet come to terms with the divine gift of language, although we know from experience the power a single word can have. The cry "Fire!" can set in motion a stampede of thousands of people; the word "Stop!" can pile up cars for a mile. Language, however, has a value far beyond what such instances suggest. For language is the divine instrument placed at man's disposal for bridging every gap, opening every vista, plumbing the depths of all created things, and interpreting the deepest insights of man's spirit. But we must also be aware of the disclosure God makes of Himself, and has made, in the world, and particularly in the life of every individual.

The ability to express adequately what we see and feel, what we think, do, and know, is exceedingly limited in the case of most people, even the well-educated. Is it unfair to say that this is eminently true in the area of prayer? Very few Christians can find the words to say what they profess to believe about God, about Jesus Christ, about the Holy Spirit, about the Church, or forgiveness, or glory, or peace.

This inability plays havoc with prayer and is one of the chief reasons why we do not stay at our prayers long enough to establish the kind of relationship with God that allows Him to communicate to us His will, His love, His power, and His peace. It prevents our revealing to Him our state, our needs, our desire for Him, and our will to serve Him. We do not have the words at our command, so we do not spend the time. Inattention, listlessness, boredom, unreality, uselessness, sleep, bear down upon us—and we give up.

The only way to learn to talk is to learn to use words and to use them properly and effectively. We learn to say what we want to say, in order to communicate what we desire to make known, and to gain the appropriate response, with rather careful listening, study, application, and practice. People who use language effectively in ordinary conversation or on special occasions often find extreme difficulty with their prayers. They know the vocabulary of their profession or of refined social intercourse, and they have the skill to express themselves well. They practice it constantly, partly as conscious practice and partly unconscious. Where there is any concern for the part language plays in the total exchange of personality with personalities, people show considerable awareness of the power of the spoken and written word and of the thinking and feeling which lie behind them. Yet at prayer they fail.

Again we must say that it is not possible to pray without words. It is so important to understand this if we are ever going to bring real vitality to our praying. We simply have to master the vocabulary of prayer—the very words in which the Church's faith and knowledge of God are expressed. Our prayer is always going to be a halting and unsatisfactory expression of our relation to

God unless we revitalize it with the language of faith and spiritual perception. We have to practice learning and using in our prayer, as well as in our intercourse with people, the kind of words and phrases that express a fuller spiritual understanding of God and man and life. Words, spoken or unspoken, are the only tokens of understanding we have. That is why we hear, "What is Beethoven trying to *say?*"; "What is it that Van Gogh *says* in that painting?"; "What do those signals *mean?*" To be real, meaning and understanding require words, spoken or unspoken, conscious or unconscious.

THE VOCABULARY OF PRAYER

For the words of prayer we must turn to the Bible, to the Church's liturgy, to the written prayers of the ages, and to the books of prayers written in the language of our own day. We need to acquaint ourselves with different kinds of prayers, prayers that men and women have written for their private use and prayers that have been composed for public use. I recall a woman who was fearful for her emotional balance, asking for help because she could not pray. She wanted to pray, but confusion had stripped her of words, even of the impulse to find the words. She was given John Baillie's *Diary of Private Prayer*. "Every word seemed to say what I needed to say, what was deep in me to say, for which I could not find the way," was her word of gratitude. There are many books available that can be of similar help. This particular person used this book every day until she was able to move on to something else.

A vocabulary for one's prayer life can also be built up through reading if, while we read, we note the words and phrases that speak to our conscience, to our inner life. These words and phrases have a spiritual value for us, and sensitivity to them and to ideas which speak to our spiritual need is an opening wedge to new areas of spiritual conversation in prayer.

Words—words with their vast range of depth and experience—

34

must be learned and their use practiced. It is possible to sing many times the hymn refrain:

> "Jesus, my Lord, I thee adore,
> Oh! make me love Thee more and more"

before "adore" ever gets into our private prayer vocabulary. Then one day we are caught up into the very heart of Jesus' love—we know how merciful He has been in saving, for example, our child from shame and disgrace—and there is only one word that can say what is in us, a word we almost never use, and surely not to Jesus, and yet it comes out, "I adore You, I adore You for all Your goodness and steadfast love." No other word could say this. And while God would have known what we felt, we would still have had on our lips a silencing seal that the utterance of this word alone could break.

There is one more point—and it is an important one—that we must make about the use of words in prayer. The experience we have of ordinary, everyday life we need to continue in our practice of prayer. God cherishes long, detailed, intimate accounts of moral and spiritual experience, of possible solution of problems, of drawing out to Him the plight, as we see it, not only of other people but of ourselves. This kind of communication is essential in intimate, trusted relationships. How often have we come home from a party, an extended business conference, or a discussion about the problem of a teenager and rehearsed, either mentally or with someone in our family, the questions, reactions, situations, solutions, attitudes. Sometimes our rehearsal has marked a turning point in reaching a decision.

In the same way take your problem and lay it out before Him "who has the whole world in His Hands" and get His "slant" on it. On these occasions we do not need any special prayer vocabulary in order to present what is troubling us to God for His counsel, correction, and vision. Without speaking a single word audibly, the whole picture in its detail, grim or promising, can be set before One who we know listens intently. At such moments we become aware that even while we are revealing our inmost thoughts to our intimate Friend and Counsellor, He is talking back to us, helping us to see another side to the story, the facts we missed, the possibilities yet to be realized, our failures as well as our assumptions and convictions.

When we can have this kind of communication with God, we have left behind the childish stages of prayer. But how long we must practice for this skill, this maturity! Yet what one of us is there who can speak easily or at length about the deepest things of life? bring dignity and sacredness to the seemingly inconsequential ways of men? express his gratitude and acknowledge humbly his shortcomings and failures?

LISTENING

In ordinary life, we learn the more acceptable ways of communication by listening to those who have mastered expression and developed a facility for caring deeply. This suggests something important for prayer. It is logical that God should care how we approach Him, even as we care how people approach us. And God in Christ, through the Holy Spirit, is the Great Teacher. Jesus assures us that "the Counsellor, the Holy Spirit, whom the Father will send in my Name, will teach you all things, and bring to your remembrance all that I have said to you." (*John* 14:26)

How pregnant are these words for learning to pray. We might hark back to the emphasis on "words." Does there have to be a definite consciousness in our minds of words as an indispensable and inseparable element in teaching? "He will teach you all things." How else can "the Holy Spirit bring to your remembrance all that I have said to you" save by the specific language that Jesus uses as expression of His spirit and that is recorded for our recollection and memorizing in the Gospels? How often these words come back to us! How often they become the starting-point for opening up to God factors and features of our lives that have lain smothered, sometimes festering, over a considerably longer period than is healthy.

If we are to be taught, we have to learn to listen. Our God is a living God and He is a personal God, communicating with man in love. He has an infinitely abundant store of knowledge to reveal to us, knowledge of Himself as Father, Son and Saviour, and Holy Spirit, the Guide and Strengthener. This knowledge concerns His love and righteousness, His justice, and His peace. God is the storehouse of all we need to know concerning the creative, saving, and nurturing enterprise upon which He embarked at Creation and specifically through the life and death of Jesus, and the work of the Holy Spirit in the Church. We ought to be eager to hear this. It is the Good News He has for us. We have to practice listening to it.

This process of listening began in the early history of the Hebrews. One of the important things in the story of Adam and Eve is God's revelation of Himself in such phrases as "And the Lord God commanded the man, saying"; "then the Lord God said"; "but the Lord God called to the man, and said to him"; "then the Lord God said, 'Behold the man has become like one of us, knowing good and evil.'" (*Genesis* 2:16; *ibid.* 2:18; *ibid.* 3:9; *ibid.* 3:22) This speaking and listening encounter began early and follows straight through Abraham, Moses, Samuel, David, and eminently with the Prophets until it finally emerges in "the Word made flesh." "In the beginning was the Word, and the Word was with God, and the Word was God." (*John* 1) "The Word was God"—the word from God is God. How fruitful this is for meditation, for the background of all our listening. What He says is what He is. What God said to us, to the world in Jesus Christ, is what He is. What God reveals to us is God Himself. The words that flow and flutter in our hearts as we listen in prayer are God coming to each of us to make Himself more fully known.

It takes practice in listening to discern what Beethoven, Pergolesi, or Palestrina is saying through his music! Yet how many of us actually practice listening to God, waiting for the advent of the Spirit? What discipline that takes! What patient love and trust! This, almost more than anything else, is the secret of prayer. We tend to fling ourselves toward God with empty or passionate words that express "thanks," or plead for mercy for intolerable sins, or beg some boon beyond our power to obtain. But, oh, how seldom that patient waiting!

Our failure to do this confounds some of our converts from the Buddhist tradition, who have come from homes where faithful Buddhists have an hour for prayer and meditation in the freshness of the morning and another in the mid-afternoon before fatigue and evening diversions mutilate earnest desire toward their God!

Here lies the secret of our attending upon God. Is it learned first in the practice of assembling ourselves together for Christian worship? In our worship do we practice diligent listening to the prayers, the words of our hymns, the responsive reading of the Psalms, the regular reading of Scripture? Unhappily, ministers themselves too frequently are so concerned with "conducting worship" that they do not listen to God and interpret for their listeners what they hear Him saying in their reading of His Word and of the prayers in the Book of Common Prayer.

Is there anyone who does not know how seriously he needs to attend to what God *says* to him in worship beyond what the preacher "has to say" in his sermon? This is a place where we can begin the discipline and practice of listening to God. Is there not some correlation between the enormous ratio of absenteeism from "the assembling of ourselves together" for the worship of Almighty God and the lack of any understanding or, at any rate, a fair understanding of the necessity, value, and immeasurable privilege of listening to God as He speaks to us out of Scripture, and even while we are offering familiar prayers? It is not an uncommon experience to have one word that we see or hear speak to our moral or spiritual condition—so tellingly that we are suddenly wrenched apart from everybody and everything and hear only God's voice within us. If we are practiced in listening or desirous of learning how to listen, our participation in public worship can become an experience of refreshment, uplift, and belonging. How this can ever come about without listening is not easy to comprehend.

The act of listening is that important. Many things are involved in the practice: a spirit that desires constantly to know and to love God, an ever more chastened moral and spiritual life, frequent participation in corporate worship, and time—time to settle down, apart from everything distracting.

I can recall the instance of a loving husband who was suddenly stricken, moved to the hospital only to be confined naked, within twenty-four hours, in a solitary cell. Death followed forty-eight hours later. There had been no previous history of illness. Faithful as his wife was to Christ in His Church, she developed spells of uncontrollable weeping that continued for a week after the funeral. Her priest was called. He gave only one prescription: "You see that chair? I want you to go to it every morning for a week on the dot of nine o'clock, sit quietly and try to realize—to make real—the presence and the love of God for you. Do not get up from the chair for an hour by the clock. Do not answer the telephone; do not answer the door bell. This is time to be set apart for our Lord that He may heal you of this affliction. Let us now pray for strength for you to take your spiritual medicine." In a week she was healed of her weeping spells. Soon after she found the will of God for her, and gained the strength and the consolation to accept it.

Similar examples of progress in listening quietly to the Spirit—first at worship in church, later in the seclusion and privacy of one's own room—are numerous. It is always a matter of real wonder how the soul revives, grows, and comes to love the practice and the privilege of listening. Yet, for too many people, listening is a lost art that needs to be recaptured for life's enrichment. Nothing is more important to that discipline of life in which all life is at stake—our communion with God.

The wonderful relief from the grip of tension, the joyous assurances of God's steadying influence, the confidence in the supportive help that comes for the need of every moment, the harmony that seems to issue from the serenity that Divine Love flowing through us always gives—these are the manifest fruits of the quiet, holy converse in which our souls engage each day with God.

In summary, then, we can say: Prayer is a two-way communication between us and God. It requires detachment from the busy world, the use of words, and the art of listening. We need to pray alone and together with others, that our lives may be filled more and more with God's love for us and that we may love God more and more, and our fellow men.

3 · STRUGGLE

To imagine that Jesus Christ was not so completely identified with human life, that He did not share deeply in all its turmoil and conflict is to misread the New Testament and to miss the crucial element of the Gospel. It is of the utmost importance to keep clearly in our minds that the Master was as thoroughly related to the whole of human life as He was to the divine. This colors our whole approach to Him and to the understanding of our spiritual plight.

Prayer can be a very light matter—something "off the cuff." This kind of prayer may be what many Christians practice. And we should be realistic enough to acknowledge that many people in our time have this kind of relationship with most of the people they know, even with those to whom they bear a supposedly intimate relationship. But this is life at its most superficial, and we must not think of prayer in those terms. "Saying prayers," "reading prayers," getting down on our knees and rattling off the Lord's Prayer, daydreaming in the customary posture of prayer—these are gestures in the direction of a prayer life, but they hardly begin to touch the heart of it.

Prayer is struggle, or it involves struggle. It was struggle for

Jesus—crucially so at Gethsemane, and certainly so when the power of darkness descended in all its intensity on the Cross, and He addressed the cry to His Father—and I think to Himself—"My God, My God, why hast Thou forsaken Me?" (*Mark* 15:34) To respond with weak emotion to this cry, or to the agony in the Garden, is to undercut the essential impact of Christ upon our hearts. The moment of our greatest need of Him is symbolized in the Garden and on the Cross, at the Table in the Upper Room, and in healing of people suffering desperately by the roadside (*Luke* 18:35), the poolside (*John* 5:2-7), and the wellside (*John* 4:6-12).

This is the way God meets us in prayer. This is the way so many of us come to God, pleading with Jesus to hear us and to have mercy. True, it is not that way always. Joy and exaltation, even rapture, are the spiritual atmosphere of many a devoted servant of the Lord over a fairly extended period. Often it is with such love that we respond to the pure love of God that all the sting of crisis and sin and shame are sublimated to the point of near obliteration. Praise and thanksgiving for His wonderful goodness are in the forefront. But mercy and glory and goodness are all tinged with "the subconscious awareness of the distance between life deteriorating and life potential." Midway between the darkness and the light of the life situation stands the Cross for all of us, with Jesus beckoning us, in our hesitant prayer, to the holier freedom and light which His victory over struggle has assured.

REALITY IN HIM

We are too ready to say that all this is a reality. But the greatest struggle in all prayer appears to be the effort to keep the Reality of God always before us. It must be an oft-repeated prayer experience of many to have no real sense of anybody being "on the other end of the line." Habit has possessed them. Day after day they have knelt at their bedside or flung themselves in, and "said their prayers." But a sense of reality was not even considered a necessary element. The religious gesture of kneeling, or of mood or words, was all they could contrive at the time. Preoccupation, weariness, excitement, depression, emptiness, any one or combination of them, were the principal elements of the moment. God has a definite way of making us uncomfortable with this travesty; and after a while we give up or we begin the struggle of actively reviving our relationship with Him. But this requires genuine discipline.

It is not simple to keep aware that God is real. It takes deep searching. "Truly, thou art a God who hidest thyself." (*Isaiah* 45:15) The search for God goes on chiefly in prayer. God does not throw Himself at us. The secrets of His power and love, His goodness and mercy, are not easily discovered nor heedlessly disclosed to us. Man has to strive constantly to *see* God. "The pure in heart" are promised that vision. (*Matthew* 5:8) The pure in heart are certainly those whose motives, intentions, and will are set in the direction of believing and knowing that the God whom they seek and with whom they undertake to speak is real, is there listening, hearing, loving, responding. This is truly to see God, to know Him, to feel His presence, to converse with Him, and to feel His power surging quietly but surely through mind and spirit, and often through body.

The struggle to keep God real, to keep Him consciously and visibly before us so that at all times we actually *know* we are talking to Someone—that He is there above us, around us, within us—this is unceasing in our spiritual life. How long must we bow down before we "establish contact"? How long in our prayer must we fight to leave everything behind and launch out into the deep where God is and where alone He is to be found!

> Hark, my soul! it is the Lord.
> 'Tis thy Saviour, hear his word;
> Jesus speaks, and speaks to thee,
> "Say, poor sinner, lov'st thou me?"

This is the very converse of prayer. It seems easy, simple. Haven't we always heard it that way?

Often things that are real today strangely lose their reality tomorrow. It is true of love, of knowledge, and of joy and peace. It is not that they are any less real or less true, but we dissipate the power of their reality and it vanishes from our grasp. *It takes great moral and spiritual effort to hold fast to reality.*

When you say "Our Father" is there a sudden and momentary recognition of the wonderful inclusion of *all* men in the love of the heavenly Father to whom you speak, and a certainty that He acknowledges immediately the address you make to Him? When you say "Hallowed be thy Name," are you certain that "there is joy in heaven over one sinner" who bows low in reverence at the sacred Name and who knows that God sees and hears all that we can at that moment gather up to present to Him of "the honor due unto His Name"?

How shall anyone tell another how he has striven to cope with the unreality and stalemate of prayer? how he has been led through to the knowledge that, if anything is real in life, in the relationship of spirit with spirit, and spirit with flesh, it is that occasion when, lost to everything in joy, triumph, or agony, he is face to face with His God?

Let no one think that the reality of this experience is always on an equal plane. It can't be. For there are times when God seems to hide Himself from us, to shadow His Reality. And He does this that we may the more vigorously and unrelentingly fight our way through the darkness and hard shell of our souls, through our sin and immaturity, into the tender core of His divine Spirit.

Jesus is ever the guarantor that God is a real Person. This is the crucial point for us to understand. Only in the deepest recesses of life can we give ourselves completely to another person. Something in us in every extremity demands conditions which make it possible to give ourselves completely. There must be a Person there when we pray—the perfection of the image in which we were made—who is able to accept the broken image of ourselves which we bring before Him. When I lay bare my soul, or attempt to reveal the secrets of my life, joyous or tragic,

44

I want at least to believe I am confiding in Someone who knows what I am talking about, even the far-off echoes of what I am revealing, and who has a wisdom and love beyond that which is human, to receive what I bring so unworthily to Him. I have to call Him "Father," "Saviour and Friend," and "Divine Counsellor and Guide." But He has to be a Person—three Persons, if you will, in one.

Of course He understands every language. Words are only the symbols. We put them together in neat succession, but He sees and hears words as He, being eternal, deals with days and months and years. "A thousand years in thy sight are but as yesterday when it is past, and as a watch in the night." (*Psalm 90:4*) Our strenuous effort is really one to present our life a living sacrifice to Him. This is what prayer really is, an offering and a sacrifice to God of what we are—that we may become more and more the kind of person He is, and receive more fully the eternal life that forever will be in Christ. This is our primary struggle; and reverently we can say that God on His side strives without ceasing to perfect His image in us until all that He is becomes real. This is the work of prayer on our part, and the redemptive, sanctifying love on His—this is the eternal struggle of God for man, and of man toward God.

REALITY IN US

Once we penetrate to the reality of God and the assurance that He is a personal God with whom we can have the deepest exchange of spirit, He begins to search for reality in us. This is the second phase of the struggle the soul must endure in prayer. Granted that God is real, that He is the Father of our Lord Jesus Christ, and that in a real sense we are all His children, how can all this be rescued from the vague sphere of intellectual assent or sentimental response and become translated into the reality of a deep, abiding relationship of love and vital communication for all the areas of life?

This is the ever-present problem for those who truly care about achieving the most searching relationship we can have with God and that He can have with us. This is what God strives for in us, especially through the redeeming love of Christ Jesus; and this is what we have to strive for continuously by our effort to pierce the veil of sinful flesh. It is difficult for the vast majority of Christians to sustain this real, vital relationship with God that manifests itself in loving and serving Him more than self, in praying and working toward the building of His Kingdom on earth, in allowing the Spirit to transform our weakness into strength, and to bring us to repentance for our sin. These are vital goals, and for Christians this is the core of every other relationship into which we enter. The quality and character of all that we are with all people, under all conditions and circumstances, derive from the reality of our relationship with God through Christ. Prayer is the total expression of that relationship "in thought, word and deed."

Merely to describe the scope of this interplay between God and man is to indicate something of the spiritual energy it demands. And one should not see this only from a negative point of view as though our chances of victory in the struggle were slight. They would be, let us dare to say, if our Brother had not been through the worst of the battle for us—as well as for Himself—and had not come out victorious. The struggle is not only ours, but His. We have to be "strong in the Lord, and in the power of His might." (*Ephesians* 6:10)

> Did we in our own strength confide,
> Our striving would be losing;
> Were not the right man on our side,
> The man of God's own choosing:
> Dost ask who that may be?
> Christ Jesus, it is he;
> Lord Sabaoth his Name,
> From age to age the same,
> *And he must win the battle.*

46

Our moral struggle can hardly be divorced from our life of prayer. What blinds us and prevents our seeing God is our sinful selves. What hinders the rapture and the flow of the spirit out toward God is the curve of self that never gets very far except to wrap itself again around us. It walls out the glory of God that shines in the face of Jesus and seeks the glory that we are contriving for ourselves. Herein lies the unreality of life: we strive constantly to make the emptiness of this unreality of self become the reality that is God. The encounter we have with God in prayer is His sustained effort to make Himself real to us and to expel all the trash we take out of the world's work, and to substitute nothing less than His divine Self in us.

To know in faith that we have received Christ within as we pour out our supplications and prayers—bless Him "for the means of grace, and for the hope of glory," worthily lament our sins and acknowledge our wretchedness—this is to know the touch of reality, genuine and undeniable. It is wrought not by any virtue of ourselves or through any power we have, but through the eternal goodness and mercy straight out of the heart of God.

No pious mutterings will avail in this struggle, though random words, when laden with penitence or praise, may well claim the fullness of God's mercy. The well-rounded phrases of the Prayer Book may leave us at times with only the vaguest sense of how we stand with God or of what He would say to us out of His overflowing love. But when there is struggle to find meaning in life; to realize that we are in the hollow of His hand, that our souls are hungry and thirsty for the "Bread of the world" and the "Wine of the soul," and are seeking to be free of the unworthy bondage to things and to those souls that stain our souls, then prayer can be real, communion can be genuine, change can be unmistakable.

WHOLLY INTO HIS HANDS

In the story of Jacob wrestling with "a man" (*Genesis* 32:22-32), we see one notable thing: the story of God contending with one of His servants. It lasted a long time—all night "until the breaking of the day." And at the end of the encounter, and presumably because of it, Jacob exclaimed, "I have seen God face to face, and my life is preserved." The reality of God's Presence was unmistakably imprinted upon him, and upon him came the amazing realization that his life was still his. At the end of Jesus' contention with the forces of evil as He hung on the Cross, He committed His life to God, His Father. It may be that there is as vast a difference between the issues of these two conflicts as there is between the Old Dispensation of the Hebrew faith and the New Covenant in Christ Jesus. Certainly it is one step forward in our praying to be assured that our life has been preserved from the power of the enemy. But it is quite another, and a crucial one, to struggle through prayer to the conviction that God is seeking to take our life wholly into His hands.

This is critical, because it is the true object of Christian prayer. It derives its validity entirely from our conception of the nature of Christ. It is our faith that God commended Himself to men in an absolute fashion when He took human flesh and nature upon Himself in Jesus Christ. God *became* man. He committed Himself in the man Jesus Christ to all the earthly limitations of human nature—except in one thing. With all His exposure to the sin of man, even to death caused by sin, He never Himself committed sin. It is impossible for us to conceive the scope of the inner struggle, and the outer too, which He faced every moment, "for us men and for our salvation."

The issue of His life was victory over sin and death, the great enemies of a real relationship to God, by a free and absolute commitment of all that He was into the hands of God. This is the divine cycle—God giving Himself to us and, in that giving, imploring us to give ourselves to Him. And this is the very genius of prayer. This struggle on God's side is symbolized and presented in the life, death, and resurrection of Jesus Christ, in His ascension and the descent of the Holy Spirit, and just as truly in the life of the Church, the Body of Christ. This is God's eternal gesture, the gesture that has in it ineradicable marks of eternal striving. It is His gesture for us, for our proper response and commitment to Him, to follow in Christ's way, to share in the fellowship of the Church, and to make a complete offering of ourselves in prayer and worship, in obedience to His Word, and in the denial of all the dictates and inventions of "the self wrapped around itself."

Anyone who minimizes the seriousness of this struggle, or denies its reality and virility, has a severe penalty to pay. It is the awful penalty of prayerlessness or of unreal prayer, which is mockery, as it is mockery and hypocrisy to pretend love when there is no love. Praise God if you have been spared that penalty. Praise Him, too, if for years you have allowed God to wrestle for the central place in your relationships and if you have finally succumbed to Him. If you have any compelling sense of the struggle of God for your soul, any sense of your own inner struggle to give God's redeeming love pre-eminence in your whole life, you have already become aware of the variable insinuations of the Devil for mastery in you, and the anguish of soul and body to keep him out, and the indescribable joy and release that victorious prayer to God in the Name of Jesus, and for His sake, have poured through every crevice in your moral and spiritual structure.

I tell, with permission, the story of the striving of one soul out of darkness into the light—the light of Christ. A native of Little Rock, this woman with her family of four children had somehow found her way to a seaside village near Honolulu. She was a vigorous church worker and a leader in the smaller community where she lived and in the larger community of Honolulu; her Christian influence was substantial. One day she learned that a Negro family was to occupy the rented house next to hers. Her

Southern prejudice—although she had been away five years—came to the top and obliterated Christ in her soul. She admitted as much.

The Negro family with two small children did move in, and everybody in the neighborhood looked them over. What would she do, this woman wondered, with her four small ones? The children took care of that in less than twenty-four hours—typically, they scarcely noticed the differences in color. Panic, however, reigned in the older hearts.

But on Sunday our heroine went to church—not "as usual," however. Taking "Mr. Prejudice" with her, she did not find Christ. Although a fire burned in her soul, "the Light of life" had gone out or gotten under a bushel—a bushel of terrifying sins.

For three weeks there went on these evasions, whisperings, worked-over indignation, yet, withal, a disturbing search for truth and love. Not one Sunday of the three did she hear the words of Scripture, of Common Prayer, of the hymns, or "what the preacher said." She could see and hear only the new family next door.

On the third Sunday, He came. What happened she does not know. What word dropped from the priest's mouth in prayer, what phrase of Psalm or Gospel, she could not recall. It seemed as if she had gone down into the waters of baptism and had emerged suddenly "a new creature." It was as though the darkness broke into a great dawn of love and truth and peace. It was plain—the Word from on high: "Go today, go to that woman's house—into her house—and tell her in My Name that you are ashamed and that you want to be her friend."

She went. She went that day. She would give the Devil no time to gather friends and reveal God's message and have it "trimmed to form." She knocked on the door. Her neighbor opened, and they both stood for that split second it takes for the walls of Jericho to fall down in a silent crash. One hand went out, the penitent one, strong and filled to the finger tips with the Blood of Christ—and met another, dark and warm and genuine.

"Come in," she said warmly, with all the restraint of gentle acceptance of the manifest victory for Christ between them.

"I came to tell you I want to be your friend. I am ashamed . . ."

You have probably never been in a place where a cup of coffee is the immediate and spontaneous token of complete welcome. It is that everywhere in Hawaii.

"Will you have a cup of coffee?"

I say it reverently, even though you may not understand, but doing that was almost more than offering to drink the sacrament from the same chalice.

There began that day, under the irresistible impact of God's Spirit coming straight down through "the wrecks of time," the redeeming love of Jesus in one soul who, in the strife of tongues and the anguish of body, mind, and spirit allowed Christ to crucify forever what she had only laid aside. This was a witness for Christ that walked up and down that street where everybody knows everybody else's business, and it walked steadily and without compromise.

If there appears to be in this recital, greatly abbreviated, no proper emphasis on the struggle of a soul in its ascent to God, you have misread it. Nothing but the bitterest agony in prayer, with all the fatal touch of Gethsemane, stalked through that experience. And it would be almost pitiable if, like our Master, *we* were not conscious of some similar experience with fear, jealousy, pride, suspicion, infidelity, greed, envy, malice, loneliness, anxiety, anger, or indulgence of evil desire. Not to have known something like this in a lesser or greater degree of intensity is not to have struggled with sin as Jesus indicated on the cross we *have* to struggle. If we do not plumb deeply, we only touch the fringes of God's undying and unchangeable love of us.

Someone has said, and many of us have heard Sam Shoemaker repeat it, "We lay hold of God chiefly by the handle of sin." This is a penetrating way of saying that if God sent His Son into the world to save us from our sins, the humble and penitent recognition of our sinful state sends us flying to the Cross to seek the reality of its power. Who knows another way to reach that Cross and Jesus pleading for us from it, unless we come to Him in prayer, bringing hearts and minds filled with words of gratitude and faith and love, of supplication and plea for mercy and forgiveness unto ourselves and unto all those we know have need of Him, for those who have found Him and who may be led to find Him, for the Church of Christ and for the nations and races and peoples of the world, that His sovereignty may prevail, and with it peace.

The compass of this struggle within each one of us, and also within a praying community, goes far beyond any horizon we glimpse at the outset. It involves all of us in a struggle for dominance over all traces of self-interest; it also involves us in a struggle for the strengthening of Christ's Kingdom everywhere. It is part of the eternal struggle against pettiness over against the majesty and mercy of God; against hatred and almost universal prejudice over against love, the greatest thing in the world; against all that is false and unworthy as it opposes itself to divine truth and personal honor and integrity; against war and violence to the person as opposed to "the peace that passeth all understanding." This is the compass of the human conflict: brother contending against brother and against himself; and this must ultimately become the compass of our prayer, of the total offering and commitment of ourselves that we make to God in Christ in our striving to be like Him.

WITH ALL THY MIGHT

The next great deterrent to effective and rewarding prayer is our persisting disposition toward inattentiveness. It is difficult for most of us to keep mind and heart set on God for very long, although many of us can recall long, wonderful periods of almost complete absorption into God. At those times His Love was so strong in us that we were conscious of being lifted into a divine environment that eclipsed all outward things and most of self.

These were times of long converse, times when the Holy Spirit revealed in us so much of the knowledge of Christ and the truth of God, so much direction for the way God would lead us in our particular situation, that for sheer light and power and ecstasy we could scarce bear to "come back to earth."

Yet how few, comparatively, those times have been most of us will confess with shame! The occasions when we have longed to hold close to God, but our minds have done one hop, skip, and jump after another, and our affection rambled from one inconsequential area to another, have been numerous enough to alarm us. It was not that God was far away: we were only visiting with Him in body, whereas mind and heart were fencing with first one opponent then another, until prayer had given way to interior confusion. And no matter how many times we attempted to center our affections on the God of infinite patience, the effort seemed unavailing. Superficial soliloquy took over.

This ought never dishearten us altogether. The same thing happens time and again over a book, a lecture, a concert, a business interview or while sharing in group experience. It grows out of the soil of sin, fatigue, overwhelming external pressures, and the hectic pace of so much of life today—all enemies of the soul. The struggle within to transcend their power is a tremendous one. But we must never succumb, never give up. Here, the words of the hymn:

> Fight the good fight with all thy might,
> Christ is thy strength and Christ thy right . . .

have particular, persuasive power. It is not only in the direct area of moral evil that this summons is pertinent, but in the lengthy battle that has to be waged in prayer. The Spirit never ceases to strive within us. His faithfulness is our hope. Just to trust in Him, when we have nothing but indifference, disaffection, or preoccupation to accompany our striving, is to continue to allow Him room. This is a sliver of victory which may well bring us back again and again to seek "joy and peace in believing." It is wonderful how prayer almost alone keeps us bound to Him, particularly His prayer in us.

No one knows, unless he has persisted through days and years to catch the beauty of companionship with God through Christ, how earnestly and continually one has to labor for that relationship with Him where holy conversation and the life of purity and love and truth that accompanies it bursts through repeatedly. It takes the same kind of determination and will toward perfection that nurturing love, and seeking truth, and maintaining peaceful relations, or achieving success in one's business or profession unfailingly demand. The effort and energy that go into any life enterprise are very substantial. If our aspirations are high, so are the demands upon all that we are. Time, courage, devotion, purity of intention, utter faith, and trust in the God who never fails to meet us, to wait for us, "to make conversation" and convey Himself in it—these are the elements that are integral to our spiritual struggle for power in prayer.

There is a Negro spiritual which Roland Hayes sings, and in its ethereal and plaintive way it says what thousands of words could never say with such a touch of pictorial reality:

> Lord, I want two wings to veil my face.
> I want two wings to fly away, Lord.
> Oh! Meet me, Jesus, meet me
> Meet me in the air;
> So if these two wings fail me,
> Just give me another pair.

Our helplessness in prayer, the need to soar, to fly from the chains of earthliness, and the plea for extra equipment "just in case"— here in song is the unadorned reality of the ceaseless struggle of our heart toward Him who is our All in all.

4 · FAILURE

Judas Iscariot is for every Christian a symbol of failure. The crux of his failure was his inability, despite his privileged nearness to Jesus, to break through his own resistance to the love and truth of God he saw in the One who had called him. Try as he must have, Judas could not get through to the heart of his Master. In the bitterness that only a soul in that predicament can know, he tried to crush that heart in the vain hope of relieving the torture of his own. Jesus went to His death—a death, however, that has since won many a heart broken by the failure of sin.

It is not straining a point to relate the experience of Judas directly to our life of prayer. If there is one thing every man must come to recognize in his approach to God, it is that so many times he must face—*nothing*. How else can we describe our condition when we are spiritually blank, cold, unconcerned? There are two phases to that condition: There is the absence of any desire to meet God, either to listen, to speak, or to make any conscious gesture of the spirit, toward Him; and there is that intense agony that comes when the striving soul fails to break through with anything that approaches a sense of communication. God seems withdrawn, the soul empty and blocked. The Light has gone out.

No one is ever entirely beyond such experience. Jesus' desperate cry of anguish on the cross would indicate that, for a moment at least, the burden of human sin and the impact of social degeneration almost closed away the vision of God's caring. It is not easy to put one's finger on what happens within a man when God cannot break through to draw him into some kind of communion.

CAN THE UNBELIEVER PRAY?

Many of us have known men and women who have never had any real, conscious experience of God, of His love and protection. These people, oftentimes honorable and respected, were reared in homes devoid of religion and were never exposed to the Word of God or Christian worship. They worshipped the rational, self-encrusted life. Mind and body were the orbit in which life was lived; the spirit was a vague world they did not understand. They communed with their own minds and with the minds of others and took whatever there is of direction and enjoyment from that for all of life.

What can be said to those who have had this experience? To put it simply, this can be said: God is constantly breaking through with unquestionable manifestations of His Providence, seeking communion, seeking *to communicate Himself* to all people, no matter what their spiritual heritage. God is the Sovereign Power in the world and no one is spared the impact of His moral law. God is breaking through in every instance of righteousness versus wickedness, of justice versus injustice, of mercy and compassion versus legalistic interpretations in life, of truth versus falsehood, and intelligence versus ignorance. Every time right and truth and love triumph in any human situation, God has imparted Himself and His righteous rule in that situation for men to see and know, even though they do not acknowledge the source of that revelation. If prayer is communication, then this is God's prayer to man. Whether we speak of it as "God's call" or "God's summons" or God speaking "through the experience of the race," it is what in reverse we call prayer.

This may not seem to be a compelling presentation to those who have no prior acceptance of God's ways with the world He has created. But light and movement and growth are God's unchangeable tokens of His beneficence, and they are beyond man's control. Yet man is making unbroken response to these manifestations every moment of the day. These are among God's freewill offerings to win men to the higher reaches of life where "deep calls unto deep" (*Psalm* 42:7) and where the spirit of man pierces the veil of natural phenomena and of moral law, to respond unconsciously to the God who sustains all, the Father who provides for all.

To ignore the proper development of the spiritual faculties that are given to us is to fail at life's most vital and critical point—to betray Him who gave His all for us. To be content with *our* understanding of life's meaning, to be unmoved by the supreme revelation God has given of Himself, is to fail to translate the meaning and purpose of life into the universal language of the spirit—the only language by which men live. And, fearfully, it is possible to say, it is to bring to nought the very offering God has made of His own Son for our salvation.

But man's failure is never God's failure. If the Cross says anything to Judas, wherever he may be, it says that everlastingly. God's power was communicated to Jesus unto the end, and no betrayal can defeat that purpose. God's power is still communicated to all the world, and no man's denial or rejection of it can cause it ultimately to fail. It fails only in individuals, and sometimes in particular groups, especially in those who have had no adequate opportunity to know Him as He has been revealed in His Son.

So men may not pray, but God cannot be stopped from making the wonders of His creative, redemptive, and sanctifying life manifest in them. God is always offering Himself to the whole world, through the Spirit of His Son. If we fail to respond, through ignorance or the lack of persuasive opportunity, we are still the beneficiaries of His ultimate purpose for His world. Indeed, there must be real efficacy in the prayers of the Hindu and the Buddhist—they have so much of what we can cherish as the Spirit of the Living God. They may ignorantly worship, but the seeds of goodness and beauty and love are in them. The sense of beauty, inherent and undeniable, found in the Japanese —to cite only one people—is the gift of the same God who has taught us to "consider the lilies of the field," and inspired us to offer our best skill to adorn and beautify not only our places and services of worship, but our relationships one with another.

THE CHIEF CAUSE OF FAILURE IN PRAYER

The chief cause of failure in prayer, however, is sin. That is the chief block which short-circuits our intimacy with God, and it is one of the mysteries of personality—a mystery so many of us ignore. All that is right and good and true comes from God, and is available to man in unlimited abundance—the free gift of God through Christ Jesus. Prayer is the channel through which God makes all that He is available to us, according to His Will and our need. But fear, lust, greed, doubt and all the host of the enemies of love and peace almost automatically shut us off from all that God would give us. As water fails of its proper flow when the channel is blocked, and as power fails when there is a break in the line, so pride, worry, self-indulgence, and violence break off the flow of the Holy Spirit. The spirit of man becomes dammed up; joyous outpouring is gone. Words won't come. Desire is quelled. Vision dimmed. Nearness gone. Yet we have chosen our way, and God cannot thrust Himself intimately into a soul that prefers compromise to steadfast love. He has to stand by. But the fact is that it is we who have withdrawn from service to selfishness, from submission to rebellion. The price, of course, is failure and a sundered relationship. Prayer is beyond reach.

This failure is tragic for the soul that craves the joy of its Lord. For when love fails, all fails. When the light of Christ's love goes out of the soul, it is dim indeed. Such floundering! Such "beating the air!" Such inner depression and anguish! This is the price God exacts. The mystery of love is in the exquisite joy and peace that are its portion—the sense of belonging, of unity, of wholeness. The mystery of hatred and betrayal and malice lies in the separation, dismay, defensiveness and insecurity they precipitate. But part of the secret of God's love is the anguish of spirit that comes of offending that love. To offend that love deliberately, time and time again, is to be truly alienated and to be caught in a false love of self and the evil self invites.

Yes, it is as possible to crush the love of God out of our inner life as it is to crush out the love of wife or child or friend. Neglect will do it. So will fear. "There is no fear in love, but perfect love casts out fear." (I *John* 4:18) Distrust, needling, accusing, berating—all these are the enemies of true love. Yet we deal in them; with the cruelty and subtle brutality of spirit against spirit, we use them as the very coin of our society. And society fails of fellowship, comradeship, harmony and understanding, because man fails to appropriate in prayer and devotion the pervasive love of God. "If we say we have fellowship with him while we walk in darkness, we lie and do not live according to the truth." (I *John* 1:6)

When our prayer fails, let us then look to our lives. When we can no longer pray, even though we have gone through the motions usually associated with prayer—kneeling, quiet, uplifted eyes or bowed head—when nothing real is happening; when it all seems wasted time and, as one person said, "so sacrilegious"; let us begin to look at the quality of our relationships, the status of our family life, our financial transactions, our regard for other people, our deep-seated prejudices. These can be real blocks to God. If these are not "in tune with the Infinite," if we are not finding truth and honor and faithfulness in them, the spirit of prayer and the spirit to seek God also wane. The more our godly relationships fail, the more that central relationship we call prayer fades.

The very way God has provided for overcoming the failures of life is that glorious and wonderful communion with Him, wherein and whereby light and strength and corrective flow into every area of life. To fail in prayer, to fail in the simplest and most fundamental relationship with God, a relationship which is not one so much of behavior as *communion,* is to court failure in our most cherished experiences and commitments. Every clergyman knows how his power fails in counselling and preaching when his inner life is all awry. Every father or mother should know how his child's basic securities are undercut when tension and strife mar the parental relationship. Failure haunts them in nearly every approach which involves the rearing of their children, and well they know the desperate efforts they make to cover and compensate for it. Harmony and understanding love are the only antidotes. Restoration of the effort to pray is the antidote for broken and confused and failing attempts to bring together the pieces of our inner structure and the way we confront people every moment.

WHAT CAN WE DO?

"I know," you say, "but how does one *at will* begin again to pray when prayer no longer has any reality?" Unless pride of a sinister sort rules us altogether, failure should drive us to seek help. Doubt that we will find it creates, of course, reluctance. We have *to will* to seek help when the odds seem to be against our getting it.

We should never underestimate God. "Ask, and it will be given you; seek and you will find; knock, and it will be opened to you." (*Matthew* 7:7) No one sees failure as clearly as God. He sees and knows all the steps that led up to our growing cold and heedless. He remembers when we first entertained the thought that it does not matter whether we "say our prayers"; it does not matter whether we confess that particular sin or not; it does not matter whether we "say grace"; it does not matter whether we go to church. He remembers how we deceived and lied and took something that did not belong to us or handled someone's body with evil intent. Always there was an accompanying suggestion of our failure—of failing parent, friend, teacher, self. The delicacy of relationship was marred, and God was there making us see it and acknowledge it to ourself, even though we tried to dismiss Him from the situation.

Everyone has failed this way at some time. Everyone! The difference, however, has almost always lain in what happened afterward. One acknowledged, it, felt sorry and said so, took it to God and asked forgiveness. The other felt the pinch, shook it off as a swimmer shakes the water out of his eyes, and went on about his business. In one case, the failure was taken over by God. This is what the Cross means, and this is why we have to take our failures straight to Him who came to give us victory over them. But in the other case, the failure went down into, what the psychologists call, the subconscious to wait there and ultimately to join other failures until at last we forgot how to pray or to want to face God straight out.

THE LAW OF RELATIONSHIP

Before, it was fairly easy to feel God drawing us to Him. Do you know what that really means? Do you understand how we are drawn to people? We see something in them that attracts us; it may be for good or for evil depending on what predominates in us at the moment—strength or weakness of character. So we are drawn to them. It is no struggle; there are no conflicting emotions. Indeed, we may be particularly drawn to be with someone because nothing cuts across our relationship. But at another time we sheepishly seek to avoid that same person because something he has done to us or we have done to him raises a block between us. This happens so often. It happens so often with us in our approach to God. It is the great secret in the breaking up of all personal relationships. Wrong-doing—deception, prejudice, disobedience, misrepresentation, disloyalty—sets up blocks and barriers in the way; we can't get over to people and they can't get through to us. When purity and love and truth and faithfulness fill our being, we find it easy to communicate ourselves to people and receive the communication they send out to us.

So sometimes it is easy to recognize that we are really and joyously in touch with God, even when we have to say to Him that we are sorry for what we have done. But when instances accumulate wherein we have failed to turn to Him, or have failed to be truthful or diligent or kind or faithful to a trust, then God is blocked off, shut out; and we not only are not able to find Him, but we do not even bother to seek Him. Something has gone wrong. God has to wait until we want Him again. And in the meantime, our whole situation tends to worsen because we are no longer drawing on the Source of all virtue and honor and goodness.

So what do we do? We have to will *even against our desire or conviction* to put ourselves in the way to find Him. "I need thee, O I need thee!" Those words, suddenly recalled from the hymn, may be enough to effect a break-through. And it is the Holy Spirit who stirs the remembrance of them. Perhaps He can't do more than that, or does not choose to. He may only want to sow a seed in the knowledge that there is enough good soil left to lay hold of it and let some roots grow. Restoration—remember it!—always begins with God. Response is left to us. Love pours out. It can be despised or felt deeply enough to bring about a turn, no matter how slight. It was only a message to a maiden and a birth in a stable that turned the world upside down. Yet it was the mighty Act of God. It is always a mighty act when the Holy Spirit breaks into a hardened heart and moves it to listen, even though it be only to the echoes of a hymn sung years ago. It is always a mighty act of God when we are given courage just to get down on our knees. It is always a mighty act of God when we heed His call enough to realize that all is not lost.

HIS MERCY AND COMPASSION

Our failure is so often God's opportunity. We have the fairly well-established idea we can handle our own lives. Seldom are we sufficiently aware that God has not built us that way. Our need of Him surpasses everything in life. Prayer on God's side, if we may speak thus of His continuous communication of Himself to us, is to establish that fact. This is the gift of faith. He undertakes to fill us with the faith that we "need Him every hour." Not to have that deep-seated faith is to tread toward failure —failure somewhere, in our knowledge of what God desires to do with our life and our knowledge of what we are doing with what we are and what we have from Him.

When faith is dim and prayer is languid or almost nil, and when restlessness and frustration walk in and out of daily experience while failure obviously overhangs, God watches so mercifully and longingly for a crevice through which He can break. It seems that His eyes have a more piercing effect when we begin to surmise that the door is closing slowly on us and shutting out the light. The less able we are to handle ourselves, the more we are driven to turn to Someone bigger than ourselves to rescue us. Maybe we can only ponder. Maybe we can only reach outward and upward. Maybe we can only hope that a way will be found. Oh! the subtle clamor of the spirit for the spirit's God, for the soul's Redeemer!

What can we do when failure stalks us, when nothing comes through, when God does not seem to care, when we know we are falling apart and yet cannot give up altogether? I firmly believe this is one of the reasons God gave us knees. We can always fall *down* before Him when we are falling *apart*, physically, morally, spiritually. This is not a play on words. It is the truth about our psychological and spiritual structure. God can do something with us when we are "resigned, submissive, meek," when we surrender our hearts and minds to Him, when we bow humbly in acknowledgment of the mystery of life and the sovereignty of his law and the absolute perfection of His love and compassion that guarantee grace and forgiveness.

The great words of Isaiah have rung through the centuries because they are true; true because they come from God, true because they are what experience teaches.

> "Turn to me and be saved
>   all the ends of the earth!
>   For I am God, and there is no other.
> By myself I have sworn,
>   from my mouth has gone forth in righteousness
>   a word that shall not return:
> 'To me every knee shall bow,
>   every tongue shall swear.'
> Only in the Lord, it shall be said of me,
>   are righteousness and strength;
> to him shall come and be ashamed,
>   all who were incensed against him.
> In the Lord all the offspring of Israel
>   shall triumph and glory." (*Isaiah* 45:22-25)

St. Paul takes up this theme in that profound passage in his letter to the Church at Philippi: ". . . at the name of Jesus every knee should bow, in heaven and on earth and under the earth, and every tongue confess that Jesus Christ is Lord, to the glory of God the Father." (*Philippians* 2:10-11)

So again: "I ask that I may not lose heart over what I am suffering. . . . For this reason I bow my knees before the Father . . . that he may grant you to be strengthened with might by his Spirit in the inner man, and that Christ may dwell in your hearts by faith; that you . . . may have power to comprehend . . . and to know the love of Christ which surpasses knowledge." (*Ephesians* 3:13-19)

"Simon Peter fell down at Jesus' knees, saying, 'Depart from me, for I am a sinful man, O Lord.' " (*Luke* 5:8)

And once again, in the oft-repeated illustration of forgiveness until "seventy times seven," Jesus Himself uses the story of a king and his servants. When the servant had a great debt he could not pay, Jesus says, "So the servant fell on his knees, imploring him, 'Lord, have patience with me and I will pay you everything.' " (*Matthew* 18:26)

Knees are magic to the soul. So are words. In each case, knees and words! If you would know the secret of overcoming failure, lay claim to scriptural suggestion and the vast treasure-house of the personal experience of multitudes who were lost and were found. Let penitence and helplessness proclaim on bended knees the need of prayer. There may be some tradition against this posture, but none that would disclaim the demand for a heart bowed down. I still have to urge that head or knees bowed down are the normal expression of failure's need of help and restoration, and that without them there is usually a citadel in the heart not yet turned over to the Lord. The plea is here repeated to those conscious of failure in their lives and in their prayer to take to their knees. There is a discipline of the eyes, ears, and fingers which ministers to victory over evil. There is a discipline of the feet suggested by the recurrence of the symbol of "walking" which runs through the Bible from Genesis (17:1) to Revelation (3:4). Nothing in my estimation can replace kneeling before God in humiliation for the ways in which we have failed Him and in cultivation of the spirit of humility, the stepping-stone to purity of heart, to the sacrifice of all that we have and are to Him, and to the selflessness that is Christlikeness. Remember, Jesus took to His knees before He took to the cross!

HOW IS PRAYER ANSWERED

One more problem must be faced before we leave our consideration of failure in prayer. What about the failure on God's part to answer our prayer? I suppose everyone has asked this question secretly, partly with shame for his lack of faith, or with some measure of disappointment, if not rebellion.

Let us be forthright enough to say that God could never answer everyone's prayers in the way they are actually put to Him. If He did so, He would be a God of great contradiction and disorder. Two conscientious captains on opposite sides of the trenches pray for victory for their forces in the impending battle. God cannot answer the form of prayer of both these warriors. Both of them may be so steeped in hatred of the enemy that God has to let the circumstances of position, geography, weather, equipment, strategy, and courage become the deciding factors while He seeks to exert His power and His love to achieve the ends of righteousness and justice in the larger problems of human relationship that characterize war.

The captains of two athletic teams appear to be in a rather different relation to God. This is either recreation or, in professional sport, industry. Again, God must be concerned with the elements in the competition which concern the total welfare of the participants. Watch two basketball teams before the first whistle blows for the start of the game. Huddled together, they all clasp hands, both hands, and those of the coach too, a seal of commitment to win. Often as they break away many of them quite openly sign themselves with the sign of the cross, a token of their commitment to One in whose hands all real victory lies. This is the climax of the offering of themselves to God that their team may win. The other team may express similarly its eagerness to win. So many of the elements of prayer seem to be manifested in such an instance, one can only think, conscientiously and sincerely.

God cannot answer the form or substance of the prayers of both teams. Pure skill and other conditions may be the deciding factors in the game. Perhaps God has answered the prayers of one group of players months before as they have offered themselves in prayer, devotion, or service to Him. But all of us know that very few athletic contests are of eternal import to God, though to us who are engaged it might seem that this particular one may be. What is of eternal import is the secret of the heart of every player. And this is what decides, if not immediately, at least ultimately, every issue in life.

God, having His hand in every issue which finally determines the destiny of every soul and of every nation, never fails to answer the prayer that He tucks away in the heart of each one of us. Our prayer fails to find the form it should take unless we listen to that "still, small voice" within. The answer God gives to our prayer is according to His prayer. We say "according to His will," but His will for us is the prayer which nestles against the walls of our heart and waits to burst forth into the thoughts that finally wing themselves into words which give meaning to all that God is unfailingly doing in us, for us, and with us. And mark it carefully, when all this bursts into the true consciousness of the soul that has found its way to God, failure for the time being is annihilated. It may be that real failure of communication may never descend upon the soul again; and if that is the case, we shall know that persistent recourse to our knees and to words struggled for, repeated from memory, read from books, can change failure into power, even as the Cross changed Jesus from "a fallen Hero" to the risen and ascended Lord of life. Especially words from the Book of books, words that withhold their meaning, but write themselves nevertheless on the heart, words that lead to other words perhaps spiritually more intelligible and transforming to us, words that are not spoken yet, except in the softer, lighter impressions on the spirit, but words that more and more take flesh and find their way into inspired acts and actions—these two, knees and words, are the great symbols of the soul's seeking for life in God.

5 · POWER

God is the source of all power in the universe, all energy both spiritual and physical. Nothing is outside His power, and no real power exists anywhere, or in anything, except it derives from Him and is sustained by Him.

There is no way to elaborate sufficiently this fundamental Christian belief in God, but it is something to ponder endlessly. Nature proclaims it every moment. The resurrection of Jesus Christ from the dead confirms it for those whose whole trust is in Him as everliving Lord of all. Our hearts remind us that "all power belongs to God" (*Psalm* 62:11), that our need of that power is unlimited, and that in Christ it is immediately available to everyone who will seek it, and is bestowed whether we seek it or not. We live altogether in the strength and mercy of it. Against this background of faith we pray. Every time we say the Apostles' Creed we declare this faith to be ours: "I believe in God the Father *Almighty,* Maker of heaven and earth."

The Bible is the story of God's mighty acts, the record of His majestic power. From the very beginning of creation to the everlasting continuation of God's rule "unto ages upon ages," the inclusive and eternal sweep of God's power is set forth. Faithful to this revelation, those who accept Holy Scripture approach God in prayer, and believe that His power, made known as infinite love and mercy, can save us.

It is in this faith that we pray. The very communication God has with us brings Him to dwell in us. This empowers us with a nature like His. We "become partakers of the divine nature." (II *Peter* 1:4) He fills us with the power of His Spirit. The power of God is about us, around us, within us, at all times whether we are conscious of it or not. It is part of God's very mercy and love for us that we do not always have to be conscious of it. It is there. He gives it to us freely. He imparts to us the power we need in food and water and air, as well as in beauty and righteousness and thought. It is His direct and loving communication with us whether we know it or care about it. It is God's side of prayer. He is in much the same relation to us as our human parents who pour themselves out, who provide and protect and care for their children, satisfying much more than their physical needs. The consciousness of trust, the emergence of love come later. And even when their children fail, their care and nurture continue.

This providence of God is the Holy Spirit praying in us. St. Paul unmistakably identifies it: "It is the Spirit himself bearing witness with our spirit that we are children of God." (*Romans* 8:16) "The creation waits with eager longing for the revealing of the sons of God." (*Ibid.* 8:19) "Likewise the Spirit helps us in our weakness; for we do not know how to pray as we ought, but the Spirit himself intercedes for us with sighs too deep for words." (*Ibid.* 8:26) "He who did not spare his own Son but gave him up for us all, will he not also give us all things with him?" (*Ibid.* 8:32) This is the way God deals with us before ever we approach Him in prayer. Indeed, it is the indwelling Spirit that instills in us the initiative, the very desire to pray. This is God praying in us, the power of God abiding in us, to bring us to spiritual birth and to raise us as need be—and the need is so continuous—"from the death of sin to the life of righteousness." This is the power from God—in us!

The response we make to the moving of God's spirit in us is *our* true prayer. And that response is laden with power, spiritual power in more than the measure of our need. The description of that response usually falls into five categories: adoration, praise and thanksgiving, confession, petition, and intercession. The full power of prayer lies in the use we make of these five kinds of prayer. We do well to explore them.

ADORATION

Who God is, even though it cannot be separated from what He does, should be our first thought of Him. For it is because of who He is that we adore Him, and this adoration is the highest form our prayer can take. If only, in childlike faith, we could say "Our Father," while having in our hearts what that truly means, all that Jesus intended it should mean, we would be truly adoring God. To allow our hearts to grasp the realization that "our" means everybody whom God chooses to call His own is to increase the compass of our spirit until "all" in God's love become the community of our love. When the soul aspires to comprehend the reality of this sublime conception of life, it enters the outer court of true adoration. When later it conceives Him as the "Father of all," who embraces all humanity, the soul veritably bursts with that strange mystical union of utter exaltation in God and knows that utter humility in its inner being that is true testimony that we adore Him.

Children have this kind of approach. Not all children, but certainly those who have had their imagination nurtured religiously. How excited they can become, with rapture and great wonder taking complete possession of their faces, when they hear a story about some noble, victorious person. I have seen God take such complete possession of little ones of nursery and kindergarten age, that when a skilful story teller vividly pictured for them God and His Son, their response was adoration of God, awareness of His very presence.

Adoration is a mature experience as well. Faith can lift us to such heights of contemplation that, in our poor way, we can say we behold His glory. Or, it may be that striving to define what God has enabled us to see of Him, we can only find adjectives and exclamatory phrases to acknowledge the impression of His spirit in our hearts: "Holy, Holy, Holy, Lord God of hosts; heaven and earth are full of the majesty of thy Glory." How little we know of what we are saying! The unspeakable holiness of God; the burning light that surrounds His dwelling-place; the glorious beauty and radiance in the face of the risen Christ, revealed so mercifully to those who see one glimpse of His wondrous self; the gentle Spirit that takes us and leads out of torturing anxiety into a place of calm and quiet peace; the near-miraculous transformation that can be found in the presence of Christ in the sacrament of Bread and Wine when in penitence and transcendent faith Christ Himself is received—here is adoration that fills the soul. Once I heard a person, by no means a fanatic, say: "It is possible, I know from experience, to become so completely lost in God's presence as to forget that I am." This makes real sense. Many a human being has such an experience in his personal relation with another where the love for the other not only completely extinguishes all selfish interest and concern, but glorifies the loved one. This is the essence of adoration; and often we can only find the words "I adore you" to satisfy the heights of emotion to which such love brings us. The child has his way of saying the same thing to his mother. Adoration, then, may be the direct response we make to the glimpse we catch of the glory of God as against our insufficiency and unworthiness—our recognition that God is due more than we can ever offer. It may be the response of our mature contemplation of His ineffable holiness, power, and love.

Can anyone ever imagine the power this puts into our life with God? To be able to offer anything like adoration is to begin to see ourselves in our rightful relation to Him. As a rule, we are more inclined to see *ourselves* as worthy of admiration than to find in another that which erases our sense of self. But the humility and selflessness that move us to adore the Triune God will generate in us the spirit of sacrifice so essential to true prayer. The power of Christ's sacrifice forces its way into the very center of our being, and we are enabled to resist the inroads of arrogance, abuse, unchastity, and malice. Even imperfect efforts to adore lessen the pull of these enemies of the soul that stem from glorification of self.

PRAISE AND THANKSGIVING

Praise and thanksgiving are very closely linked to adoration in our experience of God. It might be well to stop a moment to clarify this.

We adore God, alone for what He is. God is holy. God is loving. God is righteous and forgiving. God is our peace. He is abundant in mercy and unfailing in goodness. For all that He is, we are to adore Him and praise and glorify His Name.

But God is not only infinite and eternal, absolute and perfect, utterly righteous and holy; He has done something. He has created us, redeemed us, sanctified us, and more than that, He creates, saves and makes holy every moment among all kinds and conditions of men. For this, and for all that He has ever done and continues to do "for us men and for our salvation," we praise Him and give Him thanks. This is obvious and does not need to be labored. Not to be thankful for what is done for us is to be less than a full person. We are at great pains to teach our children from their earliest year to say "I thank you." The impulse to thank increases the range and quality of personality. It increases gradually one's acceptability and integrity. A thankless person is an obstacle to the integrity and meaning of sound group life, whether it be a family or national group. Thanklessness breathes too much of the spirit of "this is my due," "this is what I rightly deserve," "I am entitled to it."

Such a spirit has no place in our approach to God—though the attitude we appear to have too often seems to betray just that spirit. Certainly in no relation does thanklessness have positive power for good, but gratitude is always an open door to every heart.

Praise and thanksgiving must fill the heart of the man who looks out upon God's world and beholds the wonderful provision He has made for man's satisfaction. The height and depth, the lines and forms, the grandeur and magnificence and majesty of all created things, must excite one's gratitude for God's enrichment of life. True, in our present urban civilization, many are denied the insight that comes to the soul which, seeing God's handiwork in all nature, lifts heart and voice to give thanks to the Creator and Sustainer of all this beauty and glory in life. But this handiwork of God is there, nonetheless. In addition, there is health, food, and companionship, work and the opportunity to serve, home, family, and friends, and deliverance from the great dangers and evils that haunt us with their tragic threats. There is more than enough in life to excite our thankfulness.

Some of us forget that God is the source of all love and of all that is good and true and honorable. Some of us—too many, I fear—fail to give thanks to God for every blessing that comes to us, and we are made poorer by our failure. Gratitude—this special attitude of heart and mind toward the people and things around us—has power in itself to bring us rich spiritual benefits.

Love and gratitude are a universal language of the soul. They both have power within themselves to do what their opposites can never do. To lift our hearts and voices in thanksgiving to God is to come into an ever fuller knowledge of God's merciful, loving, and abundant care and concern for us; it is to have that enlargement of vision, desire, and devotion that transforms all giving and receiving, all working and serving, all sharing and helping, and makes them the reflection of God's power and love. To thank God is to begin to understand what wonderful things He has done and desires to do not only for us but for all men. It is also to release within us the power to serve as we have been served by

Him, to be so thankful to Him that we can forgive the negligence and hardness of heart of those who see not the light of His love.

It must be that God cares what response we make to Him for all that He has done for us, for He has given His Son to deliver us from all that would destroy us. If we, knowing something of that costly gift, have no concern to thank Him, what we lack thereby is *immeasurable*. Contrariwise, it must be that, if we are constantly grateful for what Christ is to us and to all men, our Saviour in every inner struggle for purity and peace, we shall know the real power there is in prayer.

CONFESSION

We come now quite naturally to consider the very special provision God has made for dealing with our moral and spiritual lapses. None of us is without them. We are all sinners. We sin against God and we sin against each other. What solution for this has God provided?

"If we confess our sins, He is faithful and just, and will forgive our sins, and cleanse us from all unrighteousness." (I *John* 1:9) Here then is the special ordinance God has made whereby our sins may be done away: repent and be whole again. Without repentance we remain outside the gracious promises of God. True, lasting communication with another is impossible without specific regret for the mistakes, neglect, indifference, annoyance, pretense, or misunderstanding for which we are responsible in that relationship. Regret or, as we say, contrition, our sorrow for failure, is not quite enough. If there is a sincere desire to cultivate and keep the relationship vital and rewarding on both sides, we must *acknowledge* that regret, or contrition, first secretly to ourselves, then openly to the other person. "I am sorry" are the magic words for restoring a marred relationship, whether they be said because we accidentally bump into someone or because we have seriously offended someone. If the reason for the "I am sorry" is immediately and clearly evident, that is tantamount to an open confession. If the word or deed which marred the relationship is not obvious, it becomes imperative to acknowledge the fault specifically, to indicate our sorrow and our desire to avoid a repetition of it, and to restore in every way possible all that may have been lost by what we did.

We are in exactly this situation with God, who in His mercy has made this wonderful provision for counteracting the devastating effects of our wrong-doing. He has made it so that when we sin, true communication is thereby broken and cut off. This is the price that we must pay for sin and misdeeds—for evil desire, evil thought and design, and all other offenses. To those who do not know the miracle of God's love in Christ, He has even provided that in our common social intercourse the words "I am sorry," genuinely spoken or indicated by some appropriate apologetic gesture, are usually effective for restoring the broken relationship.

How much more wonderful it is when we confess our sins to God to know that He gave His only Son to take these sins unto Himself on the cross for all mankind. And as though that were not enough—and it really is not except we understand the all-inclusive scope of that love—He puts it into our heart not only to confess deeply, sincerely, precisely, but to make every possible effort to forsake that sin in the future, to act toward Him or the offended person or persons in a redeemed way, and to make such restitution as we may.

This spiritual package that we call *repentance* has confession at its core. The whole package gives to the penitent, as he confesses his sin, total release from sin's tentacles.

I am, as I have urged, a firm believer in the power of words in every prayer situation, and none more than in confession. There is a special power in being explicit about our sins. God knows every detail of our life and every ingredient and choice that went into our committing a particular besetting sin. Part of our failure in prayer is our corrupt tendency to gloss over the real essentials of evil in us, or in the situation we contrived, when we face up to God in our confession. We want some covering phrase, some generalization, to minimize and counteract the awfulnes of our sin in His sight.

When someone has seriously hurt us, how we lie awake or walk around with it, spelling it out in all its vivid details to ourselves, or worse, to another over the back fence or the telephone or the sink, adding to the facts whenever our resentfulness and chafing lead us to do so. But when we, in our guilt, come to say to God in prayer what we know to be enormously evil with a firm hold on us, with complications, implications, and involvements for others that are wide and hurtful—our fear, malice, jealousy, prejudice, passion, intemperance, wastefulness—we too often dismiss that sin with a gesture of thought, a phrase or two that does not encompass what God expects us to say about it. We do not clearly, precisely, pictorially, formulate that sin before us in fairly accurate, grammatical construction and, therefore, with compelling power.

So we have to take a long, searching look at our sins on occasion. (But not continuously, lest we become sentimental or morbid about sin.) This kind of examination takes time. And that is why we go into our room and shut the door to be alone with God when we want to review our soul's state before Him and to receive the full power of His forgiveness and the strength that will flood in upon us so that we may return to the wicked world we know awaits us, refreshed and able to resist its open and hidden traps, as well as to meet its glorious prospects. The assurance for this confident return to the world comes from deliberate reporting of our sins to God, after which comes the mysterious sense of full cleansing and forgiveness. What greater power is there for renewed attack on life than this?

PETITION

We now move naturally to the fourth kind of prayer experience. We call it *petition*. It would appear from most of the questions which are asked about prayer and from the doubts which are expressed about it, that asking God for what they desire constitutes the prayer life of most people and their concept of what prayer is.

This is a costly mistake, for petition is only one kind of prayer and, in a mature spiritual life, never takes first place. There is, I think, one exception: If our asking is for the great spiritual gifts which God wants all His children to have in abundance, then there is never enough of this glorious asking we can make. Such asking, however, will be so shot through with adoration of God, so full of praise and thanksgiving, and of acknowledgment of our unworthiness to receive anything except through the grace and pleading of Jesus that, by the inspiration of the Holy Spirit, we shall seek only those profitable things which God would have us ask for.

God is Love. Imagine for a long moment the power of God's love—embracing everybody and everything in this world. Imagine the scope of Jesus' love as He willingly gives Himself for all men that they may have the power to forsake their perversions and to find love and truth and goodness and the peace of God. Do you think God wants our lives to be filled with love? Jesus rebuked His disciples for not allowing the children to come to Him when they wanted to do so and felt drawn by His love. If the disciples had really understood the power of His love, how quickly they would have brought the children into His divine presence.

Indeed, is there a greater need today in our conflict-ridden world than the need for love? Yet, do we pray every day for love? Do many pray constantly for that greater love that can make a man lay down his life for his friends? (*John* 15:13) Would not such prayer also lead us to pray for a love of truth and make us more honest and truthful in all our relationships? And should we not also pray to be rid of all fear, anxiety, and worry? *There is no fear in love.* Our fear of people, of our enemies, of the future, of failure, of death, would rapidly diminish, even disappear, if faithful to the love of Jesus, we prayed for the power and grace of

77

God's love in every circumstance and relationship. Could hatred, prejudice and nationalism, divorce, juvenile delinquency, and industrial strife, survive if men were to pray for the love that God yearns to give, yearns so much to give that His Son died to show us that love?

Love is only one of God's manifold gifts, but it is the first. It has a transforming power without equal over the whole of God's creation. And prayer is the key that unlocks it for our every need. Love is the one virtue which, when found strong and true in a home, satisfies and fulfills every bodily, mental, psychological, moral, social, and spiritual need. But the true power of it to meet every exigency of life lies in the way it is linked to God's love, derived from it, and supported by it. And it is in prayer that we bring God to bear on these exigencies of life—prayer that seeks purification, renewal, and an ever more inclusive extension, until the beauty and witness of love are shared as widely as possible for God's sake, who makes it continuous and everlasting.

What is said of love can also be said, in the same context, of all God's gifts for His children. Wisdom, knowledge, righteousness, justice, reverence, obedience, sacrifice, purity of heart, forgiveness, generosity—all these and more must be woven into our prayer time and time again, hour after hour, as we commune with God, seeking from Him what we need for the fulfilment of His will and purpose for us.

It is in the true spirit of prayer to recognize that God knows all our needs before we ask, that He knows the spiritual need that lies behind our asking. Likewise, He knows the material needs for which we have also to ask: daily bread, a sphere of work, bodily health and strength. He knows our need to ask for protection from all physical dangers. It is constantly in my thought that these needs are always provided by God in His own way according to our true need. What we need chiefly to pray for are the spiritual gifts, and to thank God always for the bread and meat that come from honest work. To say this is only to say what Jesus said: *But seek first his kingdom and his righteousness, and*

78

all these things—what you will drink and what you will eat and what you will wear—*shall be yours as well.* (*Matthew* 6:33)

INTERCESSION

The fifth kind of prayer we call *intercession*. The important point about intercession is that we should not for one moment come to God for ourselves alone. Prayer that does that is a result of a sinful focus on self and an almost unconscious commitment to physical self-preservation. We ought always to remember that the first law of our spiritual nature is this: *Whoever would save his life will lose it and whoever loses his life for my sake will find it.* (*Matthew* 16:25; also see 10:39; *Mark* 8:35; *Luke* 9:24 and 17:33; and *John* 12:25.) We have to give our life away in the strength of God's grace to other people, for other people, and for the sake of their life and welfare. We have particularly to "take them to God in prayer."

One woman, a conscientious Christian social worker with an absorbing love for people in need and trouble, once said she was so busy presenting peoples' lives and dire circumstances to God every day, she had no time left to ask Him for anything for herself. Insofar as it can be literally true, this is to lose one's life for Christ's sake and know that the more one prays for others' needs, God gives us the power to meet both our needs and theirs. If it were not true, there would be an increasing lack of anything substantial to give those whom we would serve in Christ's Name.

The needs people have are basically spiritual needs. And poverty, we know, is a mighty enemy of the soul—particularly poverty such as characterizes our mechanized civilization. To realize this, we have only to think of the slums with their endless trail of taverns, the ever-constant threat of unemployment, the widespread curse of hunger, the lack of decent housing, the scourge of war, and the ever-presence of tragedy. When we kneel before God in prayer, we should present to him the needs of the people who must endure these privations and sufferings. There are probably some who will tell you that food, clothing, and shelter will not come to these people as a result of your intercession for them in prayer. Ah! but they do—provided we humbly relate their *physical* and our *spiritual* needs. For, even while we pray for them, God awakens in us a new social conscience that enables us to rise from our prayer with an empowered vision of what can be done. Or, He raises in our midst new leaders in the man's age-long struggle for justice and righteous dealing. But more than that, God looks to the spiritual needs and gives us the power to rise from prayer with new understanding and concern for the neighbor whom in prayer we have learned to love.

In our intercessions we need to pray first for the Coming of the Kingdom. And just as we cannot confess our sins without remembering that every sin we commit involves at least one other person and normally many more, neither can we pray for the coming of the Kingdom of God without remembering that no kingdom exists without people, and certainly not the Kingdom which Christ came to establish. We remember that to pray for the kingdom of righteousness and justice and peace, the kingdom where

> The wolf shall dwell with the lamb,
>> and the leopard shall lie down with the kid,
>> and the calf and the lion and the fatling together,
>> and a little child shall lead them. . . .
> They shall not hurt or destroy in all my holy mountain
>>>> (*Isaiah* 11:6 and 9)

is to pray for people, for nations, races, and classes, for individuals, friends and enemies, for those we know and those we come only to hear about but who, nonetheless, enter the orbit of our heart and prayer.

What power intercession—praying for others—gives us for the service of the people for whom we pray, the people with whom we work and worship, nay, live with perhaps under the same roof. We need to pray "for our dearest and our best," as well as for those apart from us with whom our lack of intimacy impairs our intimacy with God.

What power comes with genuine prayer for those whom we do not know, about whom we have only read and heard: those who die in the air when planes collide, or who live a life of sin from which they seem unable to find escape, or who toil and sweat that we may eat and "live and move and have our being."

Oh! the power of this kind of prayer that reaches out to the ends of the earth, to the very edges of God's Kingdom where light and love have grown dim. There the Spirit slips in because we have prayed, and supports His children against odds otherwise too great. This is power for them and for us and, may we say it reverently, power for God to use in us and them, power He might not otherwise be able to exert. He has assured us in Christ that He seeks to hear our prayer to know more fully His power and His love. And because we seek Him in prayer, He is able to fulfil His prayer in us—the prayer that is His will for us and for His world.

6 · PEACE

Man needs love, deep love; he needs it in the very marrow of his bones, in his eyes, in all his nerve cells, even in the very ends of his fingers. *For man cannot live without love.*

Man needs truth, too. It must be in the very composition of his physical and spiritual structure, in his architecture, his name, his word, his promise, his agreement, his oath—society hangs on what must be true. The line, the musical note, the report, the judgment—all need to be true. Even what I believe, my faith, is a mockery if it be not true.

Man needs right! It is a miracle how early a child senses what is fair. Not yet able to distinguish phantasy from reality, preferring perhaps story to fact, yet a sense of what is right seems to be woven into the fabric of his dawning personality—a right strongly colored at first by what is right for the child and only dimly sensed; but nonetheless, a sense of right is there.

THE CROWNING GIFT

Man's peace, however, has to be won. Peace is of God, altogether and absolutely. It is His alone to give. A little quiet, a little calm are only a hint of, only a prelude to, peace. For peace is the crowning gift of God. Although it comes very late in the order of Creation, it is the first word of Redemption: "Peace and goodwill among men" or "on earth peace among men with whom He is pleased." (*Luke* 2:14) "For He is our peace." (*Ephesians* 2:14)

Instead of peace as the primary characteristic of man's relations, one with another, the very opposite prevails. Man is set against man. This is true of both individuals and groups. Jesus was very specific about this: "Then he said to them, 'Nation will rise against nation, and kingdom against kingdom; . . . But before all this they will lay hands on you and persecute you . . . You will be delivered up even by parents and brothers and kinsmen and friends, and some of you will be put to death; you will be hated by all for my Name's sake. . . . Great distress shall be upon the earth and wrath upon this people!'" (*Luke* 21:10, 12, 16-17, 23)

The story of man's life is one in which peace seems to have little place. Intended for peace, as the Creation story suggests, man has taken unto himself strife, conflict, antagonism, divisiveness, competition, oppression, warfare. The struggle against evil has been turned into a struggle against one's fellowman. "Brother will deliver up brother to death." (*Matthew* 10:21; *Mark* 13:12)

PRAYER AND PEACE

If peace is the crowning gift of God, then it must also be the final goal of our life with God, the very spirit of all our prayer, and the genius of our prayer life. This is an inescapable conclusion. Peace with God is the sure reward of faithful, humble, ceaseless prayer. It must be the final fruit of love and righteousness and truth, but especially of the love that leads us into all that is right and good and true.

To understand this as thoroughly as we may, we must now look into the theology of prayer as it bears particularly upon the peace of God, the peace which God gives through Jesus Christ, as we respond to Him in the offering of our whole self, our total experience of life, and the compass of the world as we are able to discern it spiritually.

It seems to me that peace hinges, above all, upon the cardinal principle of responsibility. "In the beginning God created the heavens and the earth." (*Genesis* 1:1) ". . . and God saw everything that he had made, and, behold, it was very good." (v. 31) God took responsibility for Creation and for all that He had created, the visible and the invisible. True, a flaw developed: "The serpent beguiled me." (3:13) And man, God's highest creation, acknowledges his imperfection. In spite of God's perfect handiwork, man turns out to be not "very good."

God takes responsibility for this, too. This is part of the perfection of God. For how many aeons God labored to bring man back into the realm of perfection which He had intended, no one knows; but "when the time had fully come, God sent forth his Son . . . to redeem those who were under the law." (*Galatians* 4:4-5) Here is the complete assumption by God of full responsibility for what He had initiated in creation. The way is opened in Christ for the perfecting of all who accept adoption as sons.

RESPONSIBILITY AND PEACE

Every conception we have of the human father-son relationship includes and requires acceptance of responsibility on the part of the son as well as the father. The conception we have of divine Fatherhood and divine Sonship is the same. So Jesus takes complete responsibility as the Son of God for the salvation of all men from the effects of man's initial departure from the divine purpose. But because He is Son of man as well as Son of God, He passes on to man an inescapable destiny of moral responsibility, and—I believe we may say—spiritual responsibility. Although God unquestionably takes total responsibility for His world and for every individual creature He has made, including

84

man, and man especially as His noblest creature—a responsibility which embraces the total life-experience of each one of us—God puts upon man partial responsibility for what he becomes.

The meaning of this responsibility lies in the meaning of the very word itself—the ability "to respond or answer for one's conduct." Here, by implication, is suggested the problem of freedom versus determinism. Practically all Christians, and a large percentage of scientists not actually committed to the Christian religion, hold to the principle of moral responsibility.

The theme of this book holds to the scriptural position of responsibility—namely, that man has a spiritual responsibility to God that is summed up in the life of prayer. God approaches man in His responsibility not only as Creator but as Redeemer and Sanctifier. The responsibility He assumed is immediate in every moment of experience. Likewise, God asks that man's responsibility to Him shall be in every moment of experience.

If he were completely able to fulfil this responsibility, man would live in perpetual peace. Though God never fails to bear His complete responsibility at every point in the universe and in the individual soul of each of His children, we do not bear ours; and that failure mars our peace. Our defiance of the will of God disturbs, upsets, confuses, and unbalances our relationship with Him and with, we might justly say, the whole of creation. We become irresponsible. We are not able to relate in the way God intends to anybody or anything in God's world.

God does not leave us in that predicament, however. His responsibility is complete and eternal. When we fail in our moral and spiritual responsibility, *we are still offered a means of restoration, the channel of prayer*. We can look to Him and be saved. We can acknowledge our guilt—the warning bell of separation and failure in bearing our responsibility—confess our sins, receive the forgiveness of God, be transformed into His likeness and find *peace*. Thus God provides us with a means for assuming our portion of responsibility for the fulfilment of the divine will.

THE FIRST STEPS TOWARD PEACE

We are driven to seek peace by the truth and righteousness within us. We can't abide the frustration, turmoil, insecurity, and guilt feelings that filter into our whole being, our whole world of experience. An insistent demand rises within us to resolve them, and the ultimate resource is prayer—prayer for the peace of forgiveness, for the grace to respond to Christ and to unite ourselves with God. This is peace.

We have to translate all of this into our actual experience in prayer. No one of us is exempt from the struggle with evil. No one of us can respond to the movement of God's Spirit within us without a terrifying sense of the evil within us. We do not need to exaggerate. God's holiness and glorious perfection confront us with such a sense of what we might and should be, with such a sense of transgression, that we have no fullness of joy and peace. And this awareness of God's presence and perfection is not a static thing. It is not something we merely say about Him. It is something which possesses us, energizes, draws, and projects us at the same time—draws us into an even fuller realization and knowledge of God as true Father, Saviour, and Guide, and projects us into a further realization of the possible moral and spiritual responsibilities we could and should assume "for His sake."

When this happens, the lines are drawn. God is offering us peace. The human will come to grips with the divine will and the stake is peace. Spiritual experience teaches that, no matter what the consequences to submitting to God's will, to accepting the responsibility for forsaking the old man who is so insistent in us, and for accepting the new man—no matter what these consequences, to accept that responsibility is to find peace. St. Paul puts it vividly: "The God of peace will soon crush Satan under your feet." (*Romans* 16:20)

PEACE AND THE BROADENING
OF PRAYER

In this personal encounter with God, when He strives to resolve, on His behalf and for our sake, the ever-present conflict with evil and sin, not only is there the solid question of personal responsibility and peace, but also the larger question of taking responsibility for Christ's work, the redemption of society. "Blessed are the peacemakers, for they shall be called sons of God." (*Matthew* 5:9) Here bursts upon us the principle of spiritual responsibility. "Sons of God!" with solemn responsibility to the Father for "making peace!" St. Paul says of Jesus' role or responsibility: "He is our peace, who has made us both one, and has broken down the wall of hostility," creating "in himself one new man in place of the two, so making peace." (*Ephesians* 2:14-15)

It is impossible to avoid the implication of larger responsibility which the disciples of Christ have thrust upon them by this reconciliation. With the peace of Christ bestowed by reason of our personal obedience to God's will, and the formation in us of a new man and a new life, we are sent out to confront the world. Responsibility moves into a wider area.

As this is written, one of the major issues in our world is nuclear testing. This issue is the very epitome of current conflict. Yet four men in a little ketch have become the symbol of peacemaking, and have attracted world-wide attention. Why? Because by attempting to sail into the very danger zone of nuclear testing in the Pacific, they were ready to lay down their lives in order to witness for peace. The publicity they have gained may fade. Yet it is unlikely that their effort at peace-making will have no influence on the conscience of the nation, for their testimony is in terms of the guidance of the Holy Spirit and their commitment to Christ. Prayer—prayer for the peace of the world—is their responsibility, and that prayer places upon them a responsibility to do something beyond themselves in behalf of world peace.

There is something in each one of us that precipitates conflict, clash of personality, the kind of opposition that separates. And yet the desire for unity, concord, and peace lies deep within nearly every spirit. What the world sorely needs is an enormous increase in the number of people who pray constantly, daily, for peace, the peace that will resolve their own inner conflicts, the peace that may come to those whose inner conflicts spread out to confound and harass almost indiscriminately, the peace that God would bring to the nations and races and classes of people the world over. No Christian can assume a greater moral or spiritual responsibility than this, for all the love and truth and goodness that Christ brought into the world leads but to "the peace that passes all understanding." In a war-torn world and a conflict-centered society, the righteousness and truth and love which do not lead ultimately, through prayer and union with Christ, to peace and have their aim set on peace must fall far short of the mark of Christ. For purification there is always the need of that prayer that "seeks peace and pursues it." (*Psalm* 34:14)

PEACE AND RECONCILIATION

And again, the true genius of peace is reconciliation. How largely the religious concept of this special work of God is written into the very basis of our faith! St. Paul writes of Christ Jesus, "For in him all the fullness of God was pleased to dwell, and through him to reconcile to himself all things, whether on earth or in heaven, making peace by the blood of the Cross." (*Colossians* 1:19-20) How much of all our prayer should find its roots in this profound revelation ought not to be hard to recognize. The fullness of God, reconciling all things, making peace by the Cross! This is our Gospel, the very heart of our faith in Christ.

The secret at the heart of this Gospel is none other than that of responsibility. When we begin to pray that peace may come, it is man's failure to respond to God and the demands of His Kingdom in the world which should mostly engage us. As God gives us the grace to assume that responsibility, His gift of peace will descend upon us and upon our world.

The element that is uppermost in the divine process of reconciliation is that of transcending differences and conflicts. An extreme, but justifiable, interpretation of this conception is the doctrine that God Himself could not communicate Himself to man fully before Christ came because of the vast difference between Creator and creature. The whole of the Old Testament can be read in the light of this suggestion. "The fullness of God was pleased to dwell" in Jesus, and only as God communicated Himself to man fully in the Son of man, and only as man could comprehend and, therefore, communicate himself intelligently "through Jesus Christ our Lord," could reconciliation of the differences between the divine and the human be achieved. This is the basis of our truest approach to God. "You who were once estranged and hostile in mind . . . he has now reconciled." (*Colossians* 1:21-22) Strangers: This tells the secret of life. David prayed, "We are strangers before thee and sojourners, as all our fathers were." And hear also St. Paul to this point: "So then you are no longer strangers and sojourners, but you are fellow citizens with the saints and members of the household of God, built upon the foundation of the apostles and prophets, Christ Jesus himself being the chief cornerstone, in whom the whole structure is joined together and grows into a holy temple of the Lord; in whom you also are built into it for a dwelling place of God in the Spirit." (*Ephesians* 2:19-22) One has to remember that St. Paul's commission as an Apostle was to break down the wall of difference between Jew and Gentile and, thereby, in Christ make peace between them. We are the great inheritors of that Gospel which he expounded.

None of us can escape being confronted with the vast differences God in His wisdom has provided. Nature is the everlasting herald of them. No one can ever exhaust its variety and variation. So it is with man. No two people in the world alike, and yet there is a similarity that makes possible a ground for reconciling every difference and conflict.

This is, at one and the same time, a motive for praise and a motive for confession of sin. It is to the glory of God that there is no sameness in His creation, yet enough similarity and difference to give proper vitality to all experience. It is to our discredit that we take the glorious differences that God has wrought among us and make them the ground of hostility, envy, malice, covetousness, jealousy, and distrust. Yet we never quite escape, in mind or conscience, the divine necessity to find the peace God has given in Christ Jesus. The reason we must love our enemies is that peace may ensue. The reason we must deal righteously is that the foundations may not be destroyed. (See *Psalm* 11:3) All our prayer is hampered, if not vitiated, by our failure to understand this.

THE BARRIERS TO PEACE

Differences in God's sight make for His glory and ours. But this is a concept only prayer can give—the prayer that appropriates divine sanction and necessity for vast differences. (*Matthew* 13:30) St. Paul saw the Church as one body and the gifts of the Spirit differing widely. (I *Corinthians* 12:12-29)

All differences and conflicts are reconciled in Christ, and peace comes to those who live and pray in the acknowledgment, first of all, of the vast differences in God's world of nature, capacity, and function, and then the divine necessity for them. How wonderful it is to pray constantly and witness unceasingly to faith in the unity, harmony, and concord that have been wrought by Christ Jesus, and the privilege we have of the inner peace He has given those who live and pray and labor for the coming of the kingdom of peace.

This spirit cultivates for us such relations with all people as God has cultivated in us. What a story a priest on the Lower

East Side of New York City tells of the almost desperate effort to reconcile the gangs and the individuals in the gangs to Christ and His Church, to each other, to their community, and to the decencies of society, and the right relationships between the sexes.* What if all Christians had this problem of deprived youngsters on their hearts, and, out of the reconciling love of God in their own hearts, worked and prayed lovingly for understanding and cooperative effort instead of ostracism and a punitive philosophy toward them; there might then come eventually a saving peace.

Down in Montgomery, Alabama, God raised up out of abiding love and continuous prayer an apostle of peace. And the world came to see a young Christain minister, imbued with the seemingly irresistible power of Gandhi's kind of peaceful procedure, again supported immeasurably by prayer, prayer and love together in one great unity, mold 50,000 of his race in a solid witness for the racial integration of public transportation. Indeed, it was from prayer that Gandhi himself derived his power for the good of his people.

For twenty-five years and more, I have prayed every day for peace, using a special prayer. The more I have prayed, the more war-minded the world has become, the more have blown the winds of war, hot and cold. This has never brought dismay because I have known that other thousands were also praying. I am sure they were not dismayed, either.

God wants us to pray for peace. He wants us to pray for peace and to work for peace. The prayers that men have offered for the reconciliation of differences in ideology, political philosophy, and economics, as well as in international relations, are being answered in the upsurge of people's hearts everywhere for peace. The United Nations is an answer to peace prayer. Only God could have caused such an organization to come into being for the work of better understanding and greater mutual as-

* C. Kilmer Myers, *Light the Dark Streets* (Greenwich: Seabury Press, 1957).

91

sistance among nations and all sorts and conditions of men.

This international effort in behalf of world-wide peace and disarmament should be the subject of unceasing prayer. Always, God is communicating His reconciling Spirit in every conflict and in every adventure for peace. He recognizes the differences in national groups and in their philosophies. He has made most of them out of the stuff of creation—climate, geography, and innumerable elements of environment, tradition, history, and experience. All these differences are reconcilable because Christ Jesus has broken down the basic partition and has made it possible in His Spirit to find the way to harmonize the differences.

PEACE—NO MISTY IDEAL

As I have prayed for the peace of the world through all these years and have seen strife on a world-wide scale increase, the fruits of prayer have ripened in my life in my relations with all men. And now I find myself—with every prospect of being here the rest of my life—in the Hawaiian Islands, where everything one enjoys stands in a context of impressive reconciliation of differences. There is the tourist, to be sure, who comes and goes, touching lightly, spending freely in universal vacation style, marvelling greatly at a physical and social environment to be found perhaps nowhere else, with which he can identify so easily, so casually—and without any examination, perhaps, of his sociological convictions. Here is the military, the symbol of defense against attack, that belongs and does not belong, yet because of the peaceful environment in which it sojourns, creates no threat to peace. Here too is the ever-present threat of hostility in the field of industry where pineapples and sugar reign supreme and where conflicts of self-interest can become barriers to peace. On five small islands hundreds of miles out in the ocean, the stability of two great industries has to be kept in the forefront of one's concern and prayer. One has to be here to know this, as one has to be in "the South" to know how deeply the relations between two racial groups always require a religious focus.

But the most wonderful evidence of peace here in Hawaii is that national, cultural, and racial differences are as completely reconciled as man's inclination and tendency to the sin of separateness will allow. If it is a paradise—and it may be called that—it is not primarily because of the inimitable climate, nor the mountains and ocean within a few miles of each other everywhere on all the islands, nor the flowers and trees which for variety and color and abundance can be matched in few places and almost mystically suggest "the beauty of Thy peace." It is rather because of the reciprocal acceptance and amazing disregard of racial and national differences. It is not universal, but neither is it superficial or mere accommodation. It is the genius of the place, and proclaims the manifest intent of "God in Christ reconciling the world unto Himself." Here the colors of skin run the gamut from white to black. The Hawaiians themselves can be very dark. The Orientals are as different in every way as Caucasians. Beauty predominates everywhere. Dress, food, customs, traditions, and religions differ greatly. A Roman Catholic cathedral school is built directly adjoining a beautiful Buddhist temple. Through marriage national and racial strains have often been mingled indistinguishably, yet the world does not crumble, society does not fall asunder. The contributions of each group to the social whole are acknowledged, appraised, and cherished. Indeed, this is near to what the Kingdom of God might be in a secular society. It is also an environment that represents in microcosm what prayer for peace can be expected to achieve in the world. Here that goal is projected normally, vividly, and, with some reservations, structurally. This is what it must really mean to be in the Kingdom—"all one body we."

PEACE AND WORSHIP

The key to any true hope of peace lies finally, I believe, in the worship of Almighty God in His Church. The assembling of ourselves together under the guidance of the Holy Spirit for worship is God's strongest potential for peace. To be together in one place makes for a natural bond. It does in home, community, and nation. It also does this powerfully in the Church. A substantial number of differences tend to fade and, to say the least, to be temporarily ignored. This is to put it almost entirely in a negative framework, and while it is probably realistic, it is superficial, for God requires the heart in this matter as in all others.

The positive side is that the essence of true worship is so complete a spiritual focus on God and His presence by the assembled congregation as to transform a group of individuals, conscious most of the time of the differences that separate them, into a fellowship that trusts the Spirit to absorb the consciousness of those differences into a sense of unity in Christ.

This may never happen completely. But if God's unifying Presence is experienced week after week, year after year, miracles of reconciliation happen that rout sin from heart after heart, and from relationship upon relationship, until the divine begins to supplant the erring human, and the peace within begins to demand "peace with all men."

Besides this, the message borne constantly in Christian worship is, presumably and hopefully, and, by God's grace, in spite of everything, assuredly the great message of reconciliation. (II *Corinthians* 5:19) And the priest or minister who stands before the congregation as the leader of the people's worship is himself an ambassador for Christ, who has been reconciled to Christ for the ministry of reconciliation. (II *Corinthians* 5:18)

So in worship, as in other experiences in life, repetition can become the gateway to true communion, true understanding, true appropriation of character, of faith and hope and love, of truth and beauty and goodness, of strength and joy and peace. Our openness to Christ is also openness to God and the means whereby He is received, as He comes to abide in us and grow in us until we take on, more and more, His likeness and receive, more and more, His gifts of grace.

In worship, we are absorbed into Christ and the differences that our sins have made are, by His holy, spotless purity and love, taken away. The strength of them is undermined, the enjoyment of them fades; and time and again, as we come to Him with a prayer for forgiveness in our hearts, reconciliation makes us desire to be like Him, and in fact, makes us more and more like Him.

Worship is the highest form of prayer. Worship usually presumes a group "where two or three are gathered together in thy Name." This implies responsibility to God for our brother. It also implies the acknowledgment before God of the differences that exist between the two or three (and, by derivation, between all men) and symbolizes the reconciliation of those differences that has been wrought by Christ Jesus. Worship also affirms, through its very intent, the fellowship of believers, and in that fellowship, senses the absorption of all the power and purport of the evil that differences can make as they are taken up into the very life and person of Jesus Christ.

No one can truly comprehend this most glorious and wonderful encounter of the soul with God. Indeed, when our praise and thanksgiving, our confession of sin and our intercession for others and for ourselves, have together been written into the record of our communion with Him, we can only bow our heads and hearts, and receive the blessing of His peace, knowing that, at God's eternal instance, Christ has been reconciling His people to Himself.

In that peace, bestowed by God Himself alone, men go forth to do battle with the world of sin, strengthened to suffer and to die—and to rise again.